Typical fly-dressers' beasts and birds

Fly-Dressing Materials

OTHER BOOKS BY JOHN VENIARD

Fly Dressers' Guide
Further Guide to Fly Dressing
Reservoir and Lake Flies
Fly-tying Problems and Their Answers
Fly-tying Development and Progress
Modern Fly-tying Techniques

FLY-DRESSING MATERIALS

text by John Veniard
drawings by Donald Downs

with a Foreword by Taff Price

Adam and Charles Black · London

First published 1977
A & C Black Limited
35 Bedford Row, London WC1R 4JH

ISBN 0 7136 1690 3
Text © John Veniard
Line drawings © Donald Downs

Veniard, John
    Fly-dressing materials.
    Index.
    ISBN 0-7136-1690-3
    1. Title   2. Downs, Donald
    688.7'9   SH451
    Fly tying—Equipment and supplies

Printed in Great Britain by
Clarke, Doble & Brendon Ltd, Plymouth

Contents

List of colour plates

Foreword

I was more than pleased to have been asked to write a short foreword to this book, and in doing so I can repay a longstanding debt to the author, John Veniard, for without his help and encouragement I perhaps would not have tied quite so many flies and certainly would not have put my own thoughts on paper.

This book is the latest in a long line of books by John Veniard, dedicated to the absorbing art of fly dressing. It explains in detail the tools of the trade, and describes fully the feathers and fur, both exotic and more prosaic, that make up the palette of the creative fly dresser.

Every good craftsman must know his tools, and every artist be familiar with his chosen medium; so it must be with fly dressing, for is not the resultant fly a product of both art and craft? The fly dresser now has his handbook and his reference to the uses of the various feathers and furs from all over the world, including the substitutes for the rarer feathers which are no longer freely available, due to the rightful conservation of endangered species.

Today as never before more and more anglers are tying their own flies, not only to avoid the high cost of shop-bought flies, but more for the satisfaction of being able to outwit Nature herself with creations of fur and feather tied by their own hands, and to be rewarded with that inner sensation that occurs when a trout is caught by a fly of their own make and design. I rate this as being one of life's 'nice' feelings.

I am lucky enough to live quite close to the warehouse of E. Veniard in Thornton Heath and visit this Aladdin's cave often, inevitably spending more money than I intended on a rainbow of feathers (but that is part of the incurable disease of fly tying – we are all inveterate hoarders). With each visit, the magic of the warehouse never wanes and I always look forward to the next time. Now those fly dressers who live too far from Surrey to visit this warehouse can, by opening this book, experience some of the magic I feel each time I go through the door.

More than a dozen years have passed since I bought a copy of *Fly Dressers' Guide*. It rests on my bookshelf, rubbing shoulders as it were with all the other books by John Veniard forming my fly-dressing 'Bible', and I have already made space for this volume because I know it will be in constant use and be as well thumbed as its predecessors.

Sidcup, Kent   Taff Price
1977

Author's note

One of the main reasons I have never attempted to produce a book on fly-tying materials before now, is that I have included so much of this information in my previous books. In *Fly Dressers' Guide* alone there are over sixty pages devoted to materials. However, I know by the many times I have been asked, that fly tyers would welcome a book on materials, complete within itself – and, of course, not all fly tyers possess all my books.

I make this statement because much of the material contained in this book will be found in my other books, although I have done my best to make the information much more extensive and also, with the help of the coloured plates, illustrate the feathers, furs and dyed goods to a much greater degree. There is also, of course, much that is new.

I hope that by doing this I will smooth the path of many enthusiasts taking up fly tying, and also of those who have already started and who wish to take advantage of the extensive fund of information now contained within these covers.

John Veniard
1977

Introduction

Throughout the fifty years (to date) that I have been associated with the supply of materials to fly tyers, one of the major tasks has been to acquaint them, especially the beginners, with the knowledge and information needed to fill and maintain their stocks. This is, of course, due to the complexity and diversity of the items a fly tyer needs, plus the ever-changing availability of those stocks.

I think this latter aspect can be summed up, especially where the plumage of birds is concerned (the most important item of all, after the hook), in a letter I wrote in 1971 to Jack Thorndike, editor of *Trout and Salmon* magazine. This was in response to a spate of correspondence that was being conducted at the time by Richard Walker and others, concerning the rights and wrongs of tying patterns exactly to the formulae laid down by their originators.

Dear Mr Editor,

I have read with great interest Dick Walker's comments on tying original patterns, and the additional comments on the subject by other readers which have culminated in the letter by Mr W. Black of Aberdeen in January *Trout and Salmon*.

I agree entirely with the sentiments of those who maintain that original dressings should be adhered to, but I also sympathise with those who must experience the obvious difficulty in obtaining the necessary materials. Nobody is more aware of this difficulty than myself and the company I represent.

When *Fly Dressers' Guide* was first compiled, in the years immediately following the last war, it was still possible for us to draw from our stocks the items designated in the dressings given not only in my book, but also in those written and published many years before. These however, were stocks built up back in the 1920s and 1930s and when they were exhausted we had to make use of substitutes or dispense with parts of the dressings altogether. Fortunately we are still able to catch fish with the flies we tie, and I am sure none of the conservation-conscious readers of *Trout and Salmon* would wish to see rare birds destroyed merely to satisfy the exactitude of their fly tying. Nowadays, all feathers for fly tying come from birds that are reared or killed for the table, those that are 'culled' to prevent over-population, and those which are put down as 'vermin' because they encroach upon territory set aside for a specific species. In no instances are any killed specifically for fly tying on a commercial basis.

To return once again to Mr Black's letter: if one wanted to replenish one's fly-tying kit with the materials necessary to make the flies dressed in the nineteenth century, the following protected birds would have to be destroyed. Cock o' the rock, toucan, bustard, summer duck, blue chatterer, Indian crow, eagle, peacock, macaw and, of course, the last species to go on the protected list – the jungle cock. To some degree requirements are met by using the moult feathers of some birds, and the peacock is the best-known example of this. Even this bird, however, can only supply tail feathers in this manner, as it would be necessary to destroy it to get the wing and breast feathers advocated in many dressings.

Most of the feathers I have mentioned in the foregoing paragraph are used for making salmon flies of course, and immediately we refer to feathers for trout flies, the protected list is even longer.

Skues for instance, in *Silk, Fur and Feather* lists many birds that are now protected, and also some for whom the protection laws came too late. Here are some of his suggestions of the birds one should procure to provide plumage for fly tying: blackbird, great ox-eyed tit, corn bunting, bittern, bullfinch, bustard, chaffinch, cormorant, cuckoo, curlew, fieldfare, Egyptian goose, greenfinch, landrail (corncrake), skylark, martin, owl and quail (even the humble sparrow is not omitted). Swallow and swift are also included, plus the thrush, the woodpecker, the wren and the wryneck.

Happily, however, the many substitutes now introduced seem to work effectively, and I am sure that catches have been no less because a fly was tied with a feather similar, but not the same, as the one in the original dressing.

As far as ancillary items are concerned, such as tools, hooks, silks, tinsels, etc., their availability rests entirely in the hands of their respective manufacturers, so, providing they give due consideration to the needs of the fly tyer, there should be no shortage of these items.

Full knowledge of what is needed to tie flies is best gained by continually tying them, engendered of course by the continued need to obtain the necessary materials. However, not every fly tyer wishes to tie every fly in the book, or use every known material continually. Consequently, the angler who ties only for his immediate needs can never acquire as much knowledge and experience as the professional or the dedicated amateur, who ties flies as much for a hobby or pastime in itself instead of, or in addition to, his angling requirements. It is to him therefore, that this book is mainly directed, although I do hope it will be a useful book of reference for all those who are fortunate enough to discover the pleasure and satisfaction which is to be found in tying artificial flies. I have given a great deal of consideration to this aspect of the angling scene, for not only was I caught up in the fascination myself, but probably more than anyone else, I have been able to observe its influence on anglers who thought they were merely taking up a rather specialised branch of tackle making.

My more detailed observations on this will be found in the first chapter – 'How it all began' – and they are qualified by the parting remarks of one of my more elderly students on leaving an angling instructional course with which I have been associated for some years, 'Thank you for introducing me to a fascinating and absorbing new dimension of angling which I had no idea existed, although I have been fly fishing for thirty years.'

John Veniard
1977

I

How it all began

Exactly how long ago it was that the first insect imitation was fashioned we shall never know, nor whether it was just for the pleasure of deluding the fish, or whether it was necessary because of lack of a natural bait.

To reach back as far as we can, we have to consult William Radcliffe, through the pages of his *Fishing from the Earliest Times* which was puplished in 1921. He cites the writings of Claudius Aelian who lived from 230–170 B.C., and quotes from his *De Animalium Natura*. The actual extract, from Chapter 1, Book XV, is as follows:

> I have heard of a Macedonian way of catching fish (*author's note – this would set the time at about 400–300* B.C.), and it is this: between Boroca and Thessalonica runs a river called the Astracus, and in there are fish with speckled skins; what the natives of the country call them you had better ask the Macedonians. These fish feed on a fly which is peculiar to the country and which hovers over the river. It is not like the flies found elsewhere, nor does it resemble a wasp in appearance, nor in shape would one justly describe it a midge or bee, yet it is something of each of these. The natives call it Hipporus. As these flies seek their food over the river, they do not escape the observation of the fish swimming below. Now, though the fishermen know of this, they do not use these flies at all for bait for the fish; if a man's hand touch them, they lose their colour, their wings decay, and they become unfit for food for the fish. For this reason they have nothing to do with them, hating them for their bad character; but they have planned a snare for the fish, and get the better of them by their fisherman's craft. They fasten red wool round a hook, and fit on to the wool two feathers which grow under a cock's wattle, and which in colour are like wax.

There we have our first description of a fly pattern, and although the making details are of the briefest, I am sure any one of us could tie a fly from these instructions. Aelian then goes on to describe the rod used by our early fly fisherman. It was about six feet in length and a plaited horsehair line dropped from its tip. The theory expounded is that the elasticity of the horsehair made up for the stiffness of the short rod and it was thus that the fish was played and tired – the opposite of the method we use now.

From this brief description we are able to perceive the emergence of a fly fisherman and fly tyer little different in character from what he is today. He was developing a theory of imitation, dressing his flies accordingly, with much thought given to their colours, and, above all, starting the philosophy essential to successful fishing of the fly that we follow to this day. That he was conscious of the hedonistic aspect of angling with rod and line compared with other methods is summed up when Aelian says that of the many ways of capturing fish the rod, hook and line is, 'the most skilful and becoming to free men'.

The fly tyer's materials and Veniard's

As far as the materials for fly dressing are concerned, the firms who were producing the flies commercially during the nineteenth century drew their supplies from several sources, the main ones being the food markets and the millinery trade. This latter source was, of course, an ideal one, for at that time there was a very flourishing millinery industry which required large quantities of feathers for hat mounts and other decorative purposes. These included hackles, which are discussed in a subsequent chapter, the game feathers collected from the markets after the seasonal shoots, and of course the more exotic types of feather which were used for the elaborately dressed salmon flies of those times. These came from such far-away places as India, China, Africa and Malaysia, and included peacock plumes, jungle cock feathers, kingfisher, golden pheasant, Lady Amherst pheasant, silver pheasant, heron, mandarin duck, summer duck, ostrich and macaw.

The fur traders were also called upon for contributions, and from them came seal, rabbit, hare, mole and water rat fur.

The company of Veniard was founded in 1923 by the late Henry Ernest Veniard, Sen., ably assisted by H. E. Veniard, Jr. Prior to this, he had been a direct trader in animal raw materials – feathers, skins, etc. – selling to the purifiers and also to the manufacturers of millinery adornment. After 1923 he decided to concentrate on feathers alone, with the emphasis on wildfowl plumage, on which he was considered to be something of an expert.

Despite the adverse economic conditions prevailing in the 1920s, the business grew steadily, and father and son gradually expanded the field covered to include imports and exports, handling goods from all over Europe and the Far East. Prices were competitive and the going was very difficult, but Veniard's, in company with other European feather merchants, managed to carve out a share of the market.

Because of the demand created by the fly-tying sections of the fishing tackle trade it was decided to concentrate on this specialised field and, by applying a policy of fine sortings never known to the trade before, a considerable share of this business began to flow in the direction of Thornton Heath, where the Veniard business started and still operates to this day. The market, however, was bedevilled by cut prices and cheap labour, and although turnover of goods was high, profits never reached a desirable level.

Gradually commodities ancillary to fly tying (and accepted today as general fly-tying materials) were introduced – items such as varnishes, silks, tinsels and dyes. This was to serve the market which embraced individual professional and amateur fly dressers, since the large wholesale manufacturers, with up to one hundred girls to a work-room, were only concerned with raw materials.

Around 1936–7 it was decided to withdraw from the millinery feather trade and concentrate on the fishing tackle trade, so the bulk of former types of feather was gradually disposed of, leaving more time for the unique feather sortings for which Veniard's was beginning to build up a fine reputation. In fact this method of supplying feathers for fly tying is now standard practice, whereas previously all feathers were bought in bulk, and the sorting was left to the purchaser.

Because of the firm's many associations in the bulk feather business, it was possible to draw upon commodities from a very wide field, a privilege denied to competitors and subsequent imitators.

At this stage the youngest son, Frank, joined the business straight from school; another pair of hands to add to the small labour force which was now in existence.

The company was now growing steadily, and the name of Veniard became synonymous with 'quality and service' – now the company motto. No job was considered to be too large (or too small), and the business premises were kept open seven days a week for trading.

Unfortunately, the outbreak of the Second World War in 1939 brought everything virtually to a stop, and it was at least another six months before conditions returned to some semblance of normality. It was during this period that Henry Ernest, Sen., died, and H.E., Jr., shouldered the responsibility as head of the business.

With a sadly depleted staff, inadequate supplies, and the constant danger from German bombing raids (Veniard's premises are on the outskirts of London), he steered the firm on a survival course with skill and ability.

At the War's end there was a hard slog back to normal trading, and the first few years were extremely difficult, bearing in mind that Britain had been at total war for six years. Coupled with this was the great tragedy that many friends and associates in Europe had met their end in the German death camps. Despite these difficulties progress was steady, and as living conditions began to improve at home and elsewhere, business started to take on an increasing momentum. The growing interest and participation in fly fishing throughout the world also had its effect, and Veniard's began to build up to the position it has today, as the largest suppliers of fly-tying materials in the world. Larger concerns may supply and stock fly-tying materials but there are none who specialise to the same degree.

In 1964 one of the older-established firms in the trade – Messeena's – was incorporated with Veniard's and so there now exists a business with over fifty years of experience and know-how behind it. It is hoped that it will go from strength to strength.

As far as I am concerned, I grew up with the business from the age of twelve, and rejoined the firm after my military service. It was decided that I should take on a new role – that of co-ordinating the combined knowledge of my two brothers and myself in the field of fly-tying materials with my experience as a fly tyer and fly fisherman. This meant that Veniard's could give a service to their clients hitherto unavailable anywhere in the world. Because of my unique position in this field I was able to produce books, contribute to leading angling journals and make contact with anglers and fly tyers all over the world. By these means I was able to further the general interest in fly tying to a greater degree than would have been possible for any one of my contemporaries.

It has been my good fortune to make firm friends during my business activities, and also in the various organisations to which I belong, such as the Piscatorial Society, the Fly Fishers' Club and the American Federation of Fly Fishermen; the culmination, as far as I am concerned, was my being offered the Presidency of the Fly Dressers' Guild, which I was very honoured and happy to accept. Of course, many of the friends I have made can only be contacted through the medium of correspondence, particularly those overseas. This is a cause for regret, and to those whom I have not been able to meet personally and who may read this book, I would like to say that this aspect of my working life has been more rewarding than I can possibly express here. If, however, I may make a personal comment, I would say that I could not have chosen a more worthwhile section of the community to work for than anglers, and fly fishermen in particular.

To complete this background survey, I think that modern hook-makers merit an inclusion in this chapter. Without the advantage of their undoubted craftsmen's skills, fly tying and fly fishing as we know it today would be impossible. The name which springs to mind when fly hooks are mentioned is that of Alfred Partridge & Sons of Redditch, who are still producing the bulk of the fine quality hooks we are using today. Two names which are also to the forefront in this sphere are those of Bernard Sealey and Edgar Sealey, again of Redditch and cousins. Other, smaller, firms played their part, but, as is the way of modern business, they have become absorbed in larger companies. Two which spring to mind are William Bartlet of the famous 'Bartleet' hooks, and Willis (both of Redditch also), whose products were very much in demand.

Overseas companies availed themselves of the Redditch know-how and the most famous of these is within the house of Mustad whose headquarters are in Oslo, Norway. The French have a thriving hook industry, but as they also had a well-established needle-making industry their development of the hook trade followed similar lines to our own. Strangely enough, the Americans have never reached the high standards required for game fish hooks, and I think this is due to their different approach to all manufactured things. Hook-making requires a long apprenticeship to acquire an individual skill and although it results in mass-production of a kind, it is not of sufficient scale to appeal to our transatlantic cousins. In fact, it is safe to say that, in fishing tackle, good hooks are one of our major exports to the United States of America.

2

Tools

One does not require many tools to tie flies; in fact, the only accessory used in the earliest days was a pair of scissors. I know of only one fly-tying company that still ties flies in this way, and that is Rogan's of Donegal, Ireland. They are a very well-known fly-tying family, with a tradition reaching back three generations. I have no doubt that there are others who still eschew mechanical aids and gadgets, but there are few newcomers to the craft who do not start with what we now consider to be necessary items of equipment.

A pair of good scissors is absolutely essential of course, and the best kind are those with flat, slim blades and a sharp point so that we may cut our items of material close to the body of the fly. Some tyers grind down their scissor blades to a razor edge and needle point, so important do they consider this particular tool. Consequently, you will appreciate why I advocate another pair, of more robust dimensions, as these can be used for cutting quills and tinsel or other tough items without damaging the master pair of scissors.

The next important item is a pair of hackle pliers to wind our feathers round the hook shank, and here again I advocate a 'double-up' - a small pair for very soft hackles and other feathers such as partridge, and a larger pair for general hackle winding.

We need a dubbing needle for picking out fur bodies and clearing the eyes of our hooks after fly heads have been varnished and, of course, a good vice to hold the hook during the tying process. There are many vices on the market from which to choose, but, as their use is purely functional and the same in every instance (that of holding the hook in position), 'you pays your money and takes your choice'. A range of vices is shown in colour in plate 4.

Since the Second World War, many aids and gadgets have been designed to ease the path of the fly dresser, including accessories for vices on which one can hang silks and tools (as the Aird adaptor illustrated in plate 1), and the Bob Barlow gallows tool which is of great assistance when making parachute flies, illustrated in plate 2.

One of the most useful aids in my opinion is the bobbin holder. This acts as both a holder and a dispenser for tying silks, and also as a weight on the silk, holding materials in place during the tying without the necessity of using half-hitches or fiddling with a silk button. Two types of bobbin holder are shown in plate 2.

Tweezers are a most useful item as well, not only for picking up hooks and bits of material, but also for holding the fly for inspection, or when varnishing the head. These are illustrated with the scissors in plate 3.

Four more aids to complete our list are the Sheffield matched-wing pre-selector, which ensures that our wing slips will all be the same width; the Rochester hackle guard, useful when varnishing fly heads (illustrated in plate 3 with the dubbing needle and whip finishing tool); the Yorkshire wing cutter, which cuts pre-shaped wings from hackles and other feathers (illustrated with the winging pliers in plate 3), and the winging pliers themselves which are a mechanical aid for what is, to the beginner, one of the more difficult operations in fly dressing. They enable the wings to be tied squarely on top of the hook, which is essential if a neat, unsplit wing is to be formed. Moreover, they illustrate the process of tying on the wings most clearly, as it is the operational ends of these pliers which replace the finger and thumb normally used to hold the wings whilst they are being tied.

We now come to one of the most ingenious tools ever to come from the fertile minds of fly tyers – namely the whip finishing tool. As its name implies, it is used for finishing off the heads of flies and it performs its task with a speed and accuracy beyond the scope of most fingers. This ingenious little tool is of American origin and, while it is not an essential item, it will be found most helpful when it comes to finishing off a fly neatly. It imparts a whip finish which is practically invisible on small dry flies, and is just as useful for wet or salmon flies.

How long the whip finish has been with us I do not know, but I expect it goes back to prehistoric times when man first attached a blade to a handle, and must therefore be one of those simple manual operations carried out by members of the human race which has ensured its survival. It has always been a vital part of tackle making, especially for fly heads, hooks to gut or line, fixing rod rings and joining lines.

In spite of its antiquity, it was not until after the Second World War that a mechanical device was produced that would simplify the procedure, and, speaking for myself, I have used the whip finisher so often, and taught so many others its simple working, that I find it an embarrassment when I am asked to demonstrate the whip finish manually. I must emphasise at this juncture that the tool can only form the finish on an item that has no forward projection, and is therefore usable only on a fly or some other object where the whip finish is the terminal operation. It cannot be used to whip hooks to gut, or for fixing rod rings.

There must be very few people who are not aware of the simple mechanics of forming a whip finish, but for those who may be in the dark, it is made by laying the main length of silk one is using alongside the hook, or whatever, and wrapping the loop thus formed around the main length of silk *and* hook shank. After the requisite number of turns have been made, the loose end of silk is pulled tight, and the result is a 'knot' that will remain intact regardless of the most drastic treatment or passage of time.

All the whip finisher does, is to take the place of the fingers during the operation, and its metal parts being less bulky than human fingers, a more precise application can be made. One of its drawbacks, however, is explaining the procedure, but this is only because it is one of those aids that looks complex to use but is in fact easy when one knows how. With the following written instructions, and Donald's sequence of explicit illustrations, I am sure anyone could master its manipulation in a few minutes. In fact, we have proved this by handing the drawings on their own to a layman, who had no difficulty in using the tool after scrutinising them for several minutes.

Fig. 1 shows a fly tied to the stage where the whip finish has to be applied, but for practice one could use a bare hook.

Keeping the silk taut, place the curved end of the spring-loaded hook over it, as shown in Fig. 1. Now twist the nose hook under the silk as shown in Fig. 2, and take hold of the silk with it as shown in Fig. 3. The tool is now placed in a horizontal position by raising the hand, as indicated by the arrow in Fig. 3, bringing it into the position shown in Fig. 4. The dotted arrow in Fig. 4 indicates the movement we have to make to form the whip finish, and Fig. 5 shows the nose hook being revolved *round* the head of the fly, tying down the length of silk still held in the left hand. I emphasise the fact that the nose hook must be *revolved round* the hook as shown, and this is achieved by holding the handle of the tool in the forefinger and thumb, and spinning it as the arrow indicates. As a preliminary practice, and without silk or anything else, lay the handle of the tool in the palm of the right hand, and practise spinning it with the forefinger and thumb. This will also give you a good idea of how the tool operates.

Fig. 6 shows the turns of silk after they have been wound, the distance between the fly head and nose hook being exaggerated to show that it is this part of the tool which does most of the work. The object of the spring in the spring-loaded hook is to apply tension to the silk, and keep it under control at all times.

When the required number of turns have been made, drop the wrist down so that the tool is in a vertical position, as shown in Fig. 7, and give the hand a sharp anti-clockwise twist, which will release the nose hook from the silk loop, as shown in Fig. 8.

To complete the job, all we have to do now is to pull the silk with the left hand as shown in Fig. 9. This will draw the spring-loaded hook up to the head of the fly, and just before it is pulled tight, slip the hook out of the silk. A final pull on the silk will tighten the finish, and all that is now required is a drop of varnish to ensure permanence. It is important that the wrist is dropped before the nose hook is released, otherwise the turns of silk could be pulled off the head of the fly by the tension from the spring-loaded hook.

It is also important that the spring-loaded hook is slipped out of the loop before the silk is finally pulled tight, as otherwise it can be trapped and therefore difficult to remove. The two arrows in Fig. 9 show these final actions.

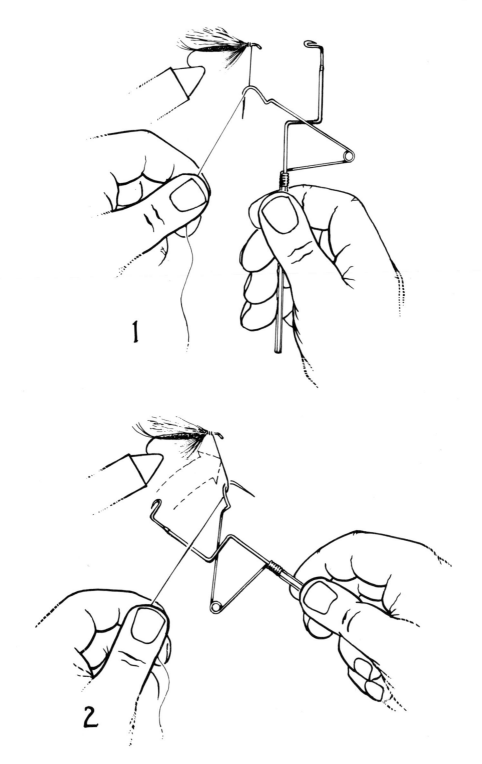

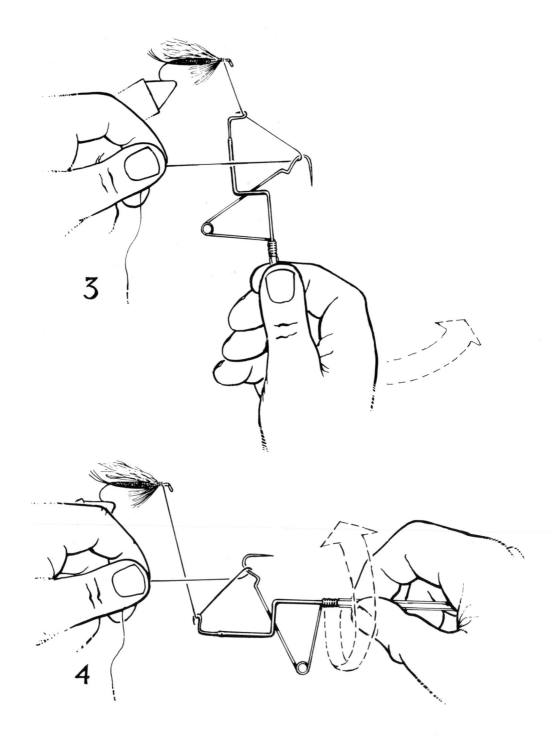

3

4

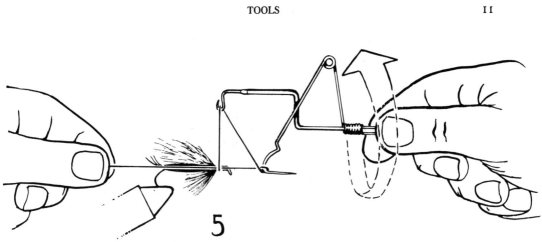

5

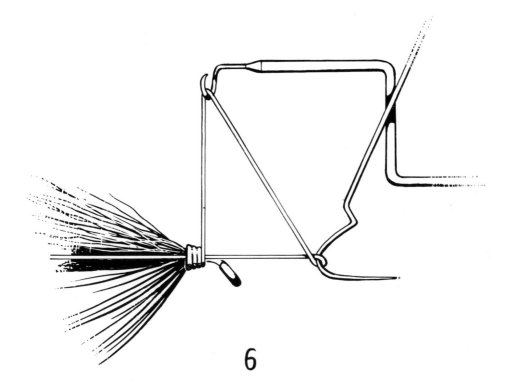

6

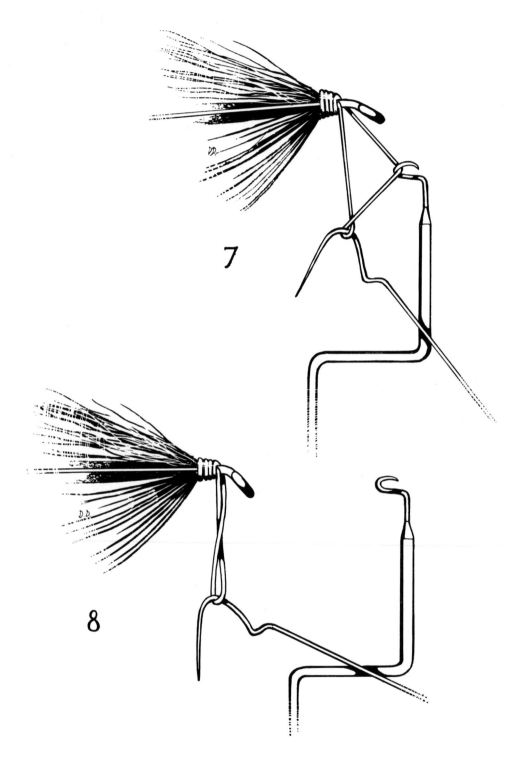

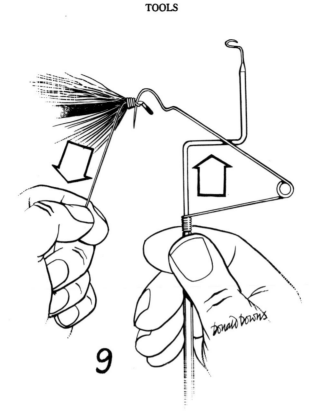

9

During the forming of the whip finish, the nose hook may be held right up to the head of the fly, but by holding it slightly away, one can apply the silk in the most precise manner, laying each turn of silk exactly where you need it. This can be most helpful when one has very little space in which to apply the turns, for instance when applying the finish to a small dry fly where the hackle is very close to the eye of the hook.

One final tip – have as much silk as possible between the nose hook and the spring-loaded hook when you start the procedure, as it is only this short length of silk (at the most $1 - 1\frac{1}{4}$ in.) that is utilised in making the turns. As I said at the beginning, making a whip finish is one of those 'easy when you know how' jobs, and the more you use the whip finisher, the more you will appreciate its accuracy and simplicity.

These tools and accessories are all that the fly tyer should ever require, although if he or she is unable to work during the hours of daylight, a good adjustable table lamp is to be recommended. Personal comfort goes a long way towards making this fascinating pastime a real pleasure.

3
Vices

Bearing in mind my comments in the last chapter, I hope you will find the following details of some use in helping you with your choice of a fly vice.

To make a vice that will accommodate every size of hook equally well presents some difficulty, and by 'every size' I mean from the smallest of trout fly hooks to the largest of salmon hooks. The reason for this is that if the jaws are cut wide enough to take the large hooks it will be difficult to close them on the small ones; and a narrow enough cut to ensure a tight fit on the small types rules out the use of the vice for large hooks. When you appreciate that hook sizes range from over 3 in. in length down to $\frac{1}{4}$ in., with corresponding differences in diameter of wire, the reason for this difficulty will be readily understood.

Furthermore, if a small fly is to be tied comfortably and well there must be no bulk of metal to interfere with the manipulation of the fingers. Therefore, a vice with a pointed nose set up at an angle is the best type to use. For a salmon fly, however, it is necessary to have plenty of gripping surface and also sufficient area of metal to cover the point of the hook.

The best design of vice combining these necessary qualities is the collet type, which operates by the jaws being pulled into a tapered sleeve to close them. Four of the vices illustrated in plate 4 are of the collet type, and they all have the attributes described, with the exception of the one with the swan neck and very small head. This is frequently referred to as the Midge vice, as it is designed to take small hooks only. The one immediately beneath it (the Northwood) is of a similar type, but it is much more robust and will also take much larger hooks. The one with the lever operation is the Cranbrook vice, and it is the lever action which draws the jaws back into the sleeve. It has a companion vice, the Ingram, which has exactly the same action, except that the jaws are withdrawn by a knurled nut (not illustrated).

The one with the double knurled nuts is the Salmo, and the best vice in the Veniard range. It has all the attributes we require, as it will take the largest hooks and the nose can also be pointed upwards for tying the smallest hooks. Furthermore, the jaws can be set at an angle so that double hooks can be tied on a level plane. The head can also be rotated during the tying of a fly, which facilitates the winding of silk and tinsel bodies (particularly on large salmon flies) and it also enables the tyer to view the fly in all its aspects during the tying. The larger of the knurled nuts at the rear tightens the jaws, and the smaller one holds or releases the head as desired. The added projection underneath the barrel simplifies the control of these operations.

All the vices shown have a solid pillar which gives both radial and vertical adjustment – movements which are regarded as standard on all modern vices – and the lever-type screws set in the clamps ensure a firm fixing in the most comfortable and useful position. A rubber button for anchoring the tying silk is also a standard fitting.

The drawing below shows a Northwood vice being used in conjunction with the Aird adaptor, and also how the adaptor can be placed into the clamp so that the jaws of the vice can be off-set to take a double hook.

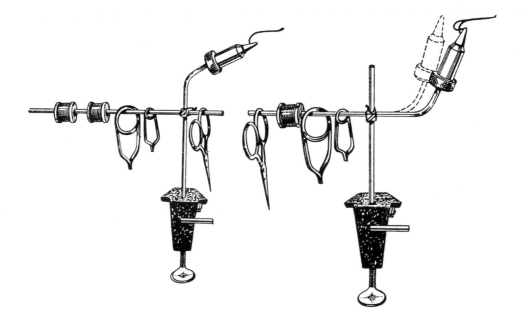

For the keen fly tyer, who wishes to tie at the water's edge when he does not have an imitation of the fly the fish are taking, there is the hand vice which is illustrated in plate 4. It has the same small collet-type head as the Midge vice, and has the advantage that it can be carried easily in a small kit of materials. It fits snugly into the hand (see drawing) and leaves as many fingers free as if one were tying without the aid of a vice!

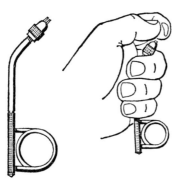

The hand vice

4

Hooks

As far as we know, the first hooks appeared around 4000 B.C., when the Ancient Egyptians were producing the earliest copper implements, tools and weapons, and it is recorded that the Chinese used iron hooks around 1500 B.C. That these were of light construction is evident from the fact that they were used in conjunction with silk lines and light, willowy rods. Previously, many other materials were used, such as bone, wood, animal claws, thorns, pieces of flint, pieces of shell and even birds' beaks. We need not delve too deeply into this era of course, but it is an interesting theory that mankind's development can be measured by the improvement made to his fish hooks.

For many centuries, the usual custom was to bind the line direct to the hook, and we do not know when 'hooks-to-gut' were first introduced. The old name for this type of terminal tackle was 'snell', and 'snelled hooks' is still a term in general use, particularly in North America. However, as far as we fly fishermen are concerned, the significant period in the evolution of the hook was the latter part of the nineteenth century when eyed hooks were first introduced. This enabled much greater scope for fly design and simplified the construction of the floating fly. Furthermore, it was the introduction of the eyed hook that made our light-weight dry fly fishing possible.

I think the main reason why some anglers complain about their hooks is that many of them do not know the characteristics of individual patterns, and the proper uses of the varied selection which is now available to them.

With modern developments there is now a hook available for every type of fishing we may want to do. Hooks are made to match the type of fish we are after, where it lives, the type of embellishment we may wish to add to it to attract the fish, and the weight of the fish we expect to catch, while being of a weight that will not deter the fish from taking it. Anyone using a fine wire hook in heavy waters where big fish can be expected is asking for trouble, just as someone using a heavy wire, coarse hook cannot expect good results in more placid and clearer waters. Put simply, no particular design of hook can be applicable to all fly fishing conditions. What we look for in all of them, however, is a set selection of attributes, and, as far as I have been able to discover, these were first propounded by the late H. P. Wells in his *Rods & Fly Tackle*, published about the turn of the century. He stated that, 'Hooks should be of good material and temper and properly enamelled (*these are the brown and black ones*) and all are to be had from good houses by paying a fair price.' The perfected description of the essential qualities of a fly hook as described by Wells, and with qualifications by Pennell and McClelland is as follows:

1 A searching (i.e. very sharp) point.
2 Quick penetration without any tendency to rake (slide across the surface).
3 Good holding power.
4 Strength.
5 Neatness of design so as to adapt itself to fly tying.

I will leave the illustrations to elaborate on the aspects of design and shape, etc., and trust that I may help in some measure to enlighten the many who curse their hook when perhaps the fault lies within themselves. I mean such hazards as over-straining the hook in the fly vice by the exertion of excessive leverage on the tying silk (particularly on fine wire long-shanks), upsetting hook temper by squeezing the off-set of a hook between the jaws of the vice, casting in rugged terrain or with a concrete dam at one's back and expecting the hook to bounce back without damage or complaint, and not examining the hook periodically when fishing under these conditions. Also, and this is a very common fault, taking a good fish and then recasting the same fly without ensuring that the hook has not been damaged during the battle. Taking into consideration the increase in the average weight of trout now taken in Great Britain, compared with the one- and two-pounders for which most of our smaller hooks were designed, I think that the hooks we use today stand up very well for themselves. This is particularly true on the reservoirs where, when conditions dictate, it is not uncommon to switch from a hefty size six lure to a lightweight size twelve or fourteen nymph or pupae imitation – and this to take the same available fish, which may be of prodigious proportions. From what other item of our tackle do we expect such flexibility?

A good hook has to have all the aforementioned attributes, look neat when incorporated into a fly, no matter what the design, travel on a horizontal plane while being fished, insert itself at the best angle for a good hold at the moment of strike, and then stay firm no matter what the size of the fish or its strength. Taking all the points into consideration, I think our hook makers do a very good job and, as they are usually qualified metallurgists, their skill and our consideration should ensure that hooks are given the respect to which they are entitled.

Having described all the qualities and attributes that we require in our hooks, this would be a good moment to give a brief description of how they are made.

Most of the manufacture in this country is carried out in Redditch, which has a long tradition in the fishing tackle trade. No doubt its needle-making activity, and the subsequent hook manufacturing which stemmed from this, is the reason why the trade still tends to concentrate in this area.

Hooks are made from high-carbon-content steel wire and, for special purposes, stainless steel wire. The first operations of manufacture are the cutting of the right

Hackle pliers

The Aird adaptor

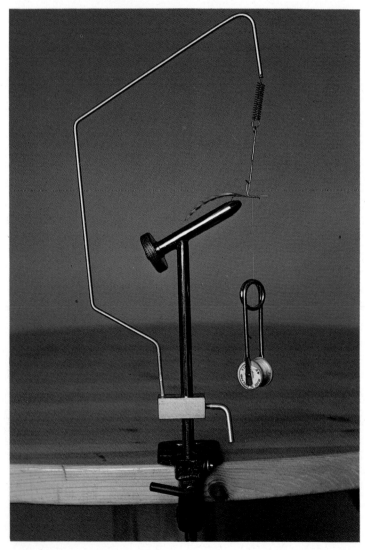

(*above*) Bobbin holders

(*left*) Bob Barlow's gallows tool

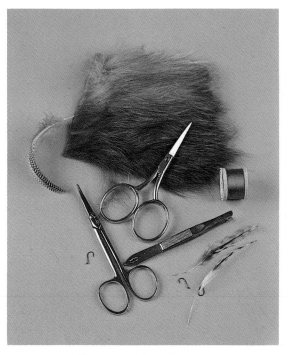

Tweezers and scissors

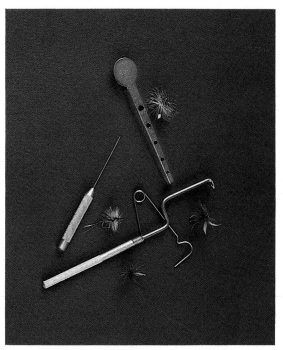

Sheffield matched-wing pre-selector, Rochester hackle guard, dubbing needle, whip finishing tool

Yorkshire wing cutter and winging pliers

(*above*) A selection of bench vices

(*left*) A hand vice

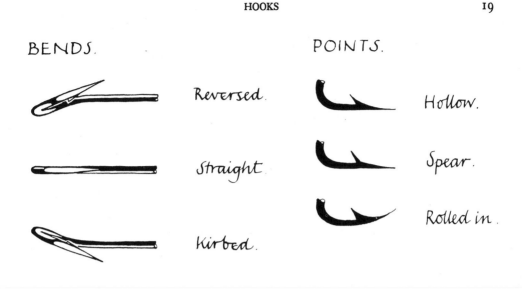

BENDS.

Reversed.

Straight.

Kirbed.

POINTS.

Hollow.

Spear.

Rolled in.

lengths, and then the pointing of the lengths on a series of carborundum wheels. Points can be either straight, tapered, or hollow-ground. The barb of the fish hook is designed to ensure a firm hold once it has penetrated and is cut and raised by a chiselling operation. This is a very important and delicate process, particularly on very small hooks. Although it was once a separate operation it is now carried out automatically by machines which also bend the wire to the correct shape and process the shank for the line attachment. Forging is carried out by automatic hammer blows which flatten the cross-section of the wire, or make it oval, as shown in the illustration on page 21.

We now come to the most important part of manufacture and the one that can be done well only by those with years of apprenticeship and experience behind them. This is the hardening, and it is done by first heating the hooks in a furnace of extremely high temperature, then cooling them by quenching in an oil bath. This process, however, merely makes the wire brittle, so the hooks must be re-heated in a slower, cooler furnace which eradicates the brittleness. This is the tempering, which completes the process of turning the original soft, malleable wire, through a brittle stage, into a tough, springy resilience. Knowing how much to heat initially, how long to quench, and how long to re-heat, are the secrets of the hook-making trade, not so much locked away in vaults or safes as in the minds and hands of those who have been taught the skills.

Of course, computerised engineering will no doubt find its place in the hook-making factories and if this should result in the production of hooks containing all the attributes I have outlined, perhaps the computer will be seen in a more favourable light by those of us who have suffered from its less successful intrusions into our lives!

The range of all types of hooks is much smaller than it was before the Second World War. If anyone then worked out a new design which the manufacturers thought practical, they were often prepared to make and market it. Such is not the case these days, as present-day costs of re-tooling, etc., make the introduction of a new pattern a costly business and therefore not a practical proposition unless very large quantities are made. However, the range of types available for fly tying is still quite extensive, and should contain suitable patterns for one's own type of fishing. The drawing illustrates the parts of the modern hook, the one illustrated being a forged upturned-eye pattern.

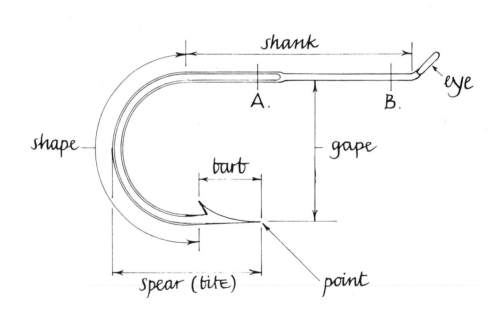

Salmon flies can be divided into four main groups: those using standard hooks which have a Dublin or Limerick bend; summer or low-water hooks which are of lighter wire and longer in the shank for the same gape; dry-fly hooks which are of very light wire and which can also be used for low-water flies, and trebles for use with the now very popular tube flies. The standard and low-water hooks are also used as doubles.

The 'shape' is the key to the hook pattern and I have illustrated one or two of the most popular. Incidentally, the 'shape' is quite often wrongly referred to as the 'bend',

SHAPES

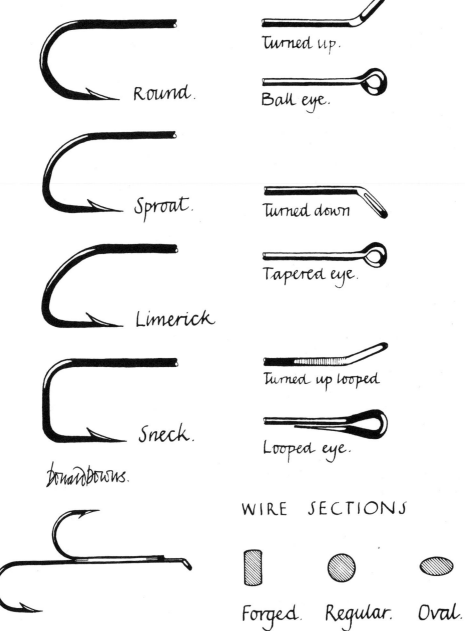

Round.

Sproat.

Limerick

Sneck.

Donald Downs.

EYES.

Turned up.

Ball eye.

Turned down

Tapered eye.

Turned up looped

Looped eye.

WIRE SECTIONS

Forged.   Regular.   Oval.

which really relates to any lateral off-set to the point and barb, i.e. when the point is off-set to the right it is called a 'reverse' bend and when it is off-set to the left it is called a 'kirbed' bend. Another misnomer is that of 'snecked' bend instead of 'kirbed', although it has been used so much now that it has become an accepted description. The purpose of these bends is to direct the penetration of the point at an angle to the shank which, as the point and the shank are not parallel, helps to prevent the release of the hook.

For dry-fly fishing, one of the best patterns to use is one with a 'Sproat' shape and turned-up eye, a slight reverse bend, and, of course, made of light wire. Second in popularity is the same type of hook but with a turned-down eye, although I think that much of its popularity is due to the fact that it is considered easier by some tyers to dress a fly on a downturned-eye hook. Hooks with this round shape are also popular for dry flies in smaller sizes, but in the larger sizes, as the wire increases in weight, they are also admirable for wet flies.

A good hook for all-round types of wet flies is the Limerick pattern, which is usually of quite stout wire. Another type of hook, which is self-descriptive, is the long-shanked. They are obtainable with either up- or down-eyes.

I am grateful to Mr S. A. Shrimpton, managing director of Messrs Allcock & Co. Ltd., for the following notes on hook nomenclature.

Bend This is definitely a trade term for the shape of the hook, e.g. a kirby bend, Limerick bend, sneck bend, etc. To shape the hook, barbed and pointed wires were pulled round on a hand 'peg-bend'; later the bend was fixed in a hand-operated machine, and the wire pulled round to shape.

As regards the different parts of a hook, we usually describe as the 'depth' that part which you call 'spear'. The machine point (as distinct from the old hand-filed point) is generally termed 'spear point' so that there should be no confusion.

In addition to the standard hook patterns, there are others that are either shorter or longer in the shank for the same gape. For instance, a Limerick No. 1X Short is one size shorter in the shank than the standard pattern, while a Limerick No. 2X Long would be two sizes longer, and so on. The smaller sizes of these long-shanked hooks are often used for Mayflies and all sizes are used for streamer flies and hair-winged lures. The theory of short and long shanks is illustrated on page 23.

It might be helpful if I enlarge on the characteristics of certain types of hooks, which readers should find of some assistance when it comes to choosing one to suit their individual purpose.

Wide-gape trout hook This is one of the few hooks that can be obtained with both up- and down-eyes nowadays. It is light in the wire, and very suitable for dry flies. It has a very slight reversed sneck, i.e. the point of the hook is set at an angle to the shank.

Gape/Length Combinations for a Typical Hook.
(Nº 8)

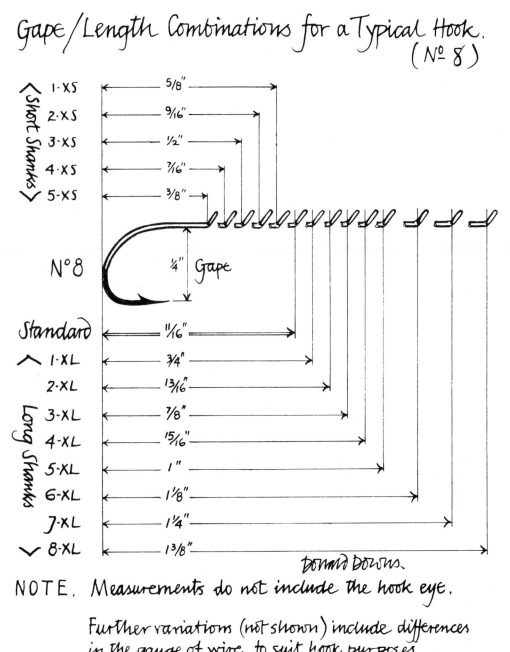

Short Shanks	
1·XS	5/8"
2·XS	9/16"
3·XS	1/2"
4·XS	7/16"
5·XS	3/8"

Nº 8   1/4" Gape

Long Shanks	
Standard	11/16"
1·XL	3/4"
2·XL	13/16"
3·XL	7/8"
4·XL	15/16"
5·XL	1"
6·XL	1 1/8"
7·XL	1 1/4"
8·XL	1 3/8"

Donald Downs.

NOTE. Measurements do not include the hook eye.

Further variation (not shown) include differences in the gauge of wire, to suit hook purposes, ie., for dry, wet & salmon flies.

Round-bend trout hooks These are used mostly for wet flies, but many anglers like to tie their small dry flies on them. They have good hooking qualities and the round bend ensures that no weakness occurs during the manufacture.

Limerick trout hooks Probably the most universally known of all the hook shapes. They are usually made in stout wire, and are very suitable for tying wet flies of the lake- and sea-trout variety.

Sneck trout hooks These are hooks with an angular bend and a slight sneck.

Ordinary forged salmon hooks This pattern is the stand-by of the salmon fly tyer, and is used for all the standard types of fly. The hooks are obtainable in a large range of sizes from about $2\frac{1}{2}$ in. to $\frac{1}{2}$ in. Double hooks in this style are not quite so easy to obtain but fortunately the need for them is not so great.

Limerick salmon hooks This pattern is used by tyers who prefer a down-eyed hook, and it also differs from the ordinary forged hook in that it is finished in bronze instead of black enamel. The scale of sizes is the same.

Wilson dry-fly salmon hooks These are very fine quality light-wire hooks specially designed for salmon dry flies. They are slightly longer in the shank than standard patterns of the same gape, so can be utilised to make very attractive low-water flies. Their strength, coupled with extreme lightness, are two features which should not be overlooked if making dapping flies for trout.

Low-water salmon hooks These are made in finer wire than the other patterns and are used for tying the lightly-dressed summer or low-water flies. They are about two sizes longer in the shank than ordinary forged hooks for the same width of gape.

Keel hook This is a very aptly named hook, as the illustration shows, and it was designed to provide a 'weedless' fly or lure without the necessity of adding extraneous guards to prevent the point and bend snagging, or having to deviate from normal fly dressing procedure. The drawing is of a Muddler type of fly and it illustrates clearly how the wing masks the point of the hook, and the upside-down method of tying the fly.

 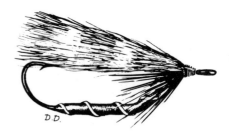

The Yorkshire fly body hook This hook derives its name from the fact that it is marketed by the Yorkshire company of Mackenzie Philps, its main feature being the difference in design from normal hooks so that it can be dressed as a 'detached body' fly. It is made in four sizes – the smallest equivalent to size 16 standard, and referred to as the 'midge size'; the 'dayfly size', which is equivalent to size 14; the 'large dayfly size' which is roughly the equivalent of size 12, and the 'mayfly size' which is about size 10.

I think the illustration of a hook and a made up fly are self explanatory.

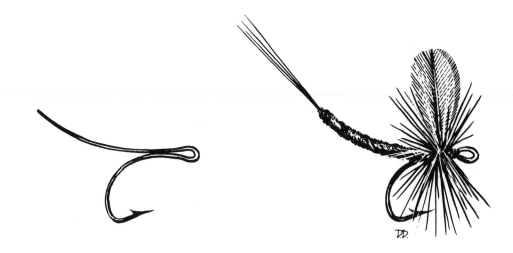

5

Silks and similar body materials

For many years, real silk reigned supreme as the material with which we fixed everything to the hook, but today it is possible to find suitable tying 'silks' in the field of man-made fibres. Whilst the nylon and terylene threads are finer than real silk, and therefore ideally suited to fly tying (particularly on small flies) their colour range is limited, and they do have a tendency to stretch. On the other side of the coin, they lie flat when wound, thus reducing bulk. But as flies have been tied successfully with silk for many decades, even on hooks in the small 20s range, and silks have such a wide range of useful colours, I think it will be a long time before they are ousted by the nylons.

For many years, the firm of Pearsall, established in the eighteenth century, has been manufacturing silk for the fly tyer, and their Gossamer and Naples tying silks and their Marabou and Stout Floss body silks are world famous. Gossamer silk is suitable for all sizes of trout flies and low-water salmon flies and, personally, I find it strong enough even for large salmon flies. However, some tyers prefer something a little stronger for large flies such as lures and salmon flies, and Naples silk fills the bill admirably.

The colour range is quite extensive, although the Naples range is a little more limited. The full list of colours is as follows. (Those not included in the Naples range are: Straw, Primrose, Amber, Light Orange, Sherry Spinner, Blue, Grey, Ash, Cardinal, Crimson, Maroon, Light Olive.)

Complete list of Pearsall's tying silks

1	White	6a	Light Orange	10	Ash	15	Maroon
2	Straw	6b	Sherry Spinner	11	Golden Olive	16	Olive
3	Primrose	7	Blue	11a	Scarlet	17	Brown
4	Light Yellow	8	Purple	12	Cardinal	18	Green
5	Yellow	9	Black	13	Crimson	19	Hot Orange
6	Amber	9a	Grey	14	Claret	20	Light Olive

For the bodies of flies, be they trout or salmon flies, silk reigns supreme, and for this purpose Pearsall's produced two types, Marabou floss which is a two-strand silk, and Stout Floss which is a heavy silk.

The two strands of Marabou floss are easily separated when cut in short lengths, and the resulting single strands are suitable for all sizes of trout flies, and the smaller sizes of salmon flies, especially the low-water variety. It holds its colour very well when exposed to oil or water, and can be obtained in the following colours: primrose, yellow, orange, red, white, black, blue, claret, light olive, olive, green, purple, brown and hot orange.

The Stout Floss is of much heavier gauge than Marabou, but just as rich in colour, and is suitable for all sizes of salmon flies and lures. It is obtainable in green, light olive, olive, light yellow, golden yellow, deep yellow, orange, scarlet, white, black, light blue, mid-blue, claret and brown.

Another floss silk produced by Pearsall's is Rayon Floss, which is a man-made fibre with a very large range of colours. It has the disadvantage that it tends to become transparent when wet or oiled, but this can be overcome by the choice of tying silk colour used underneath it. It is also fairly fine, but as it lies flat when wound, it is still possible to use it for even quite large salmon flies. If anything, it produces an even smoother body than the real silk. For very small flies, especially small nymphs of the 'buzzer' variety, it is an ideal material.

Chenille

This is a bushy material, rather like a fuzzy piece of thread; in fact it does have a silk or rayon thread core. It is very popular for large nymphs and lures, one of its attributes being that it saturates extremely rapidly, making it ideal for flies that are needed to sink quickly. It is obtainable in a very wide range of colours including fluorescent ones.

It is also now possible to get chenille that has tinsel intermingled with it, or even what is called a pure tinsel chenille. However, I think this item comes more within the category of tinsels rather than silks.

Acetate floss

Outside the range of ordinary silks and flosses is acetate floss, which has to be used with a solution of acetone. The floss is wound round the hook in the usual manner, and the acetone then applied. This transforms the floss into a malleable material which can be shaped with pliers to make any number of flat-bodied nymphs of all sizes, up to and including the large stone flies.

Tying silk - colours to use

Many dressings given in books do not state which tying silk should be used. Tinsel-bodied flies, of course, do not present much difficulty as the only place where the silk might show is at the head or through the hackle. Therefore, the colour to choose would be the colour of the hackle – black for Butcher, for instance, and red for Bloody Butcher, Red Spinner or Wickham's Fancy, and so on.

With dubbing bodies, I always use a colour approaching that of the dubbing fur used – claret for Mallard and Claret, yellow for Invicta, and olive for Rough Olive.

If a body is formed which will become semi-transparent when wet, a colour should be used which will have a neutral effect, such as white or grey.

Waxing tying silk is the initial operation in all fly tying, and although a simple process, it is a necessary one, and there is no doubt that well-waxed silk goes a long way to ensure success during the subsequent stages.

Professional fly tyers wax their silk to the extent that, even if they let go of it altogether, the adhesive qualities of the amount of wax they have applied will keep it in position and hold any materials that have been applied.

To do this, a small head of wax is kept permanently in the palm of the hand to keep it soft, and the tying silk is drawn vigorously through this so that a heavy coating is applied. This cuts out time spent on half-hitches or using weights to hold the silk and materials in place. As this consideration is not as necessary to the amateur tyer, the silk need not be treated so drastically for his needs, but it is still essential that the silk be given a good covering of wax.

The simplest way to do this is as follows: draw about 12 inches of silk from the reel (through the bobbin holder if one is being used) and hold it in place on the piece of wax by the thumb of the other hand. Now pull it very rapidly across the wax three or four times. The speed of the pull creates friction between the silk and the wax, the heat melting the latter so that it coats round the silk. The more times this is done, the thicker will be the wax coating. To pull the silk slowly is useless, for not only does the wax not melt, but the silk is prone to stick in the wax and break, or it will be weakened and break later during the tying.

One of my mentors during the early days of my fly tying, told me that if silk was properly waxed, it was not necessary to varnish the head of the fly, particularly small dry flies. I have found this to be true, but it is not an assumption I would like to lay down as a hard and fast rule. It does however, accentuate how important the waxing is, and although there is a school of thought which advocates dispensing with waxing altogether, it is not one with which I agree, if only because waxed silk is less likely to rot than unwaxed.

6

Tinsels for bodies

Tinsels are used extensively by the fly tyer for all types of flies, from the smallest dry flies to the largest salmon flies. They fulfil a dual role, in that they add durability to other body materials that may be used as well as making the fly more attractive to the fish.

There are various kinds of tinsel, all of which can be obtained in silver or gilt. They are as follows:

Flat This is a flat metal ribbon. It is sometimes used for ribbing trout and salmon flies, but is more often used when the whole of the hook shank has to be covered with tinsel. It varies in width from about one-eighteenth of an inch to one-tenth of an inch.

Embossed This is also a flat ribbon, with the addition of embossing. The embossing is supposed to impart extra 'flash' to the tinsel, but for some reason it has never been as popular as the plain flat tinsel.

Oval This is flat tinsel that has been wound round a centre core of silk, and then flattened. It is used as ribbing for all types of flies, especially lake-trout, sea-trout, and salmon. Sizes vary from about one-fiftieth of an inch to one-twelfth.

Round This is also very fine, flat tinsel wound round a siik core, but not flattened like the oval. Its main use is for the 'tag' on salmon flies, but it is sometimes used as ribbing. Obtainable in only two thicknesses of about one-hundredth of an inch and slightly less.

Twist A heavy tinsel consisting of two or three strands of round tinsel twisted together. It is used for ribbing some of the larger salmon flies such as the Akroyd, and larger sizes of some standard patterns such as the Jock Scott.

Wire This is ordinary plain drawn wire, and is used mainly for ribbing the smaller trout flies.

Lurex This is the trade name for a plastic material which has the appearance of tinsel in some instances, and which also has the advantage of being untarnishable. It can be procured in the following metallic colours: silver, gold, copper, scarlet, orange, chartreuse, royal blue, peacock blue, emerald green, and also black, white and pink. It is not as strong as tinsel, however, and a wire or oval tinsel ribbing should be incorporated when using Lurex as a body covering.

When a pattern calls for a flat tinsel body, an even foundation of silk should be wound onto the hook shank. This makes the laying on of the tinsel much easier and prevents unsightly unevenness. On large salmon flies a base of floss silk is recommended.

To the general tinsels must be added the metallic twines, the tinsel chenilles mentioned in the foregoing chapter, and also a new addition to the fly dresser's range – **Mylar.** This is a plastic tinsel obtainable in flat form, as is Lurex, and also in a plaited tubular form which makes it an admirable item for bodies, particularly those on patterns which simulate small fish. It is actually a tube of braided Mylar polyester film with a silk core and is available in either silver or gilt. There are three sizes – approximately one-sixteenth, one-eighth, and three-sixteenths of an inch, suitable for all sizes of long-shanked hooks.

The main use of the tubings is for the bodies of the streamer type of fly, to which it gives a scaled effect unobtainable with any other material. An added advantage is its simplicity in use, which entails no more than extracting the silk core from the tube and then sliding it over the hook shank.

Put in greater detail, first tie in the tail of the fly, if the dressing calls for it, then build up an under-body of floss silk, wool, or chenille according to the diameter of the tubing being used. Cut off a suitable length of tubing and remove one strand of the core with a pair of tweezers. The remainder of the core can then be removed quite easily. Slide the resultant shell of tubing over the eye of the hook, compress the end of it with the thumb and forefinger and bind it down tightly with tying silk. Repeat this at the tail end with as many turns as necessary, finishing off with the whip finish. The silk bindings should be well soaked in clear varnish, and in fact the Mylar

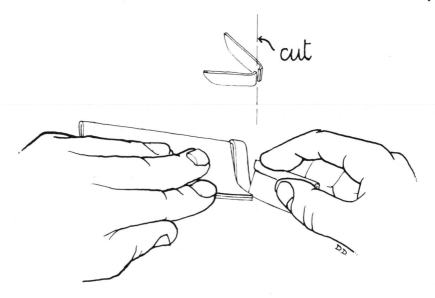

body itself can be treated in the same way for extra durability. The hackle and wings, etc. are then added in the usual manner.

It will be obvious that Mylar tubing can be used for any pattern that calls for a full-length gold or silver body, especially the Jersey Herd and other fish imitators.

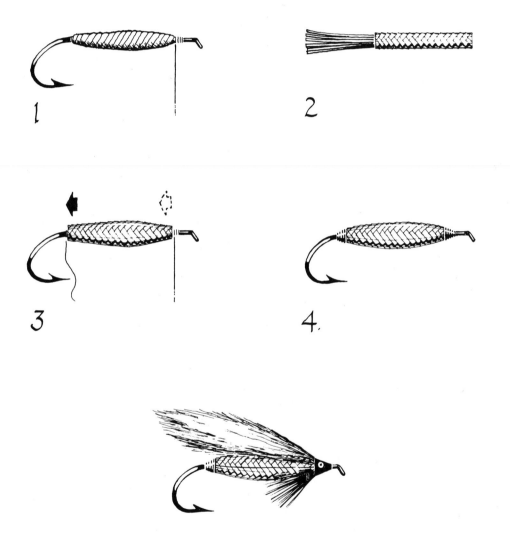

7

Body materials

We have already dealt with tinsels and silks in their separate categories, but in addition to these two essential items is an extensive list of materials one needs for bodies. They fall into three main categories: fur, herl and quill, which are now dealt with in that order.

Fur and fur-type materials

Seal's fur This is the best all-round fur for flies – dry, wet or salmon. Only fur from very young seals is used, which is cream-coloured in its natural state. The individual fibres are bright and shiny, and they lose nothing of this brightness when dyed. They do not get matted or lose their colour when wet, which is to be expected of the fur from an animal that spends most of its time in water. It can be dyed any colour, whether it be for the imitations of natural flies (Blue Dun, Olive, etc.), or the bright colours required for salmon and sea-trout flies. See plate 14.

Ram's wool This is the pink wool used when dressing Tup's Indispensable. A little natural seal's fur should be added to give it the required creaminess.

Mohair This is softer than seal's fur, but the individual fibres are very long, enabling it to be wound on like floss silk. This also can be obtained in any colour.

Rabbit fur This gives a wide range of natural colours, the most useful being the blue under-fur which is suitable for the bodies of Blue Dun, and Grey Duster.

Mole A deep smoky-blue fur that is ideal for the bodies of the Blue Dun and Iron Blue.

Hare A most useful fur from which one can obtain a wide range of usable material from one skin, ranging in colour from pale ginger to grizzled black/brown. The grizzled fur from the ears and poll supplies the body material for the Hare's Ear while the longer body fibres of similar colouring provide the hackle. It also supplies the body for many nymphs, and also that of the March Brown.

The above are the most useful to the fly tyer, but other furs which can be used are water rat, grey squirrel, brown squirrel, musk rat, etc.

In addition to the furs already listed, many body dubbings can be found at the roots of the hairs on the tails we use for winging. Squirrel tails in particular are useful for this purpose.

Polypropylene This is a dubbing material of man-made fibres, and although it comes in lengths like chenille, it can be teased out to be applied as a dubbing, and also mixed to make shades of colours. However, its main attribute is its extreme lightness (it has a specific gravity of only 0·94 approx.), which makes it ideal for dry flies, particularly the 'no-hackle' type described by Douglas Swisher and Carl Richards in their book, *Selective Trout*. It is obtainable in a very wide range of colours, including the olives and other natural colours, which can be extended further by the blending process I mentioned earlier.

Wool I do not think one need say much about wool. There is no doubt that it must have been one of the earliest materials used in fly dressing, but in most instances it has been superseded by dubbed materials such as seal fur, and latterly by polypropylene, described in the preceding section. Its main advantage of course is its availability, as the range is limitless. Its disadvantages lie in its bulkiness, and also in its tendency to change colour when wet or oiled. This is not so apparent in wools made with nylon of course, which is why it is a very popular material when fluorescent colours are called for.

Herls

The term herl is applied to strands taken from whole feathers, which are in actual fact lengths of soft quill with very short fibres or 'flue' on them. When the herls are wound round the hook shank, the short fibres stand out at right-angles, thus forming a body through which light can penetrate. The most useful come from the following birds:

Heron From both wing quills and the large hackles. Two or three strands from either of these, natural or dyed, make an excellent body, especially if a wire rib is incorporated. Very good for all the olives. (Illustrated in plate 7.)

Swan From the large, soft shoulder feathers. Being white originally, a larger range of dyed effects can be obtained than is possible with the heron, which is a smoky blue-grey. Turkey or goose make good substitutes.

Goose Also from the shoulder, very similar to swan feathers but finer. (Illustrated in plate 10.)

Ostrich These come from the large plumes and have a fairly long flue on them. They are obtainable in any colour.

Turkey The tail feathers of this bird supply many colours of herls, the most used being the brown or cinnamon for sedges, as they range from a deep brown to a pale buff. White ones dye well for nymph bodies.

Condor A very useful and very durable material is obtained from the wing quills, and can be dyed any colour. The flue is sometimes stripped, but its removal is difficult. Turkey is a good alternative.

Cock pheasant The herls in this instance are taken from the tail feathers, two or three with a wire rib forming the body of the Pheasant Tail fly. They should be tied in by the tip and not the butt, so as to incorporate the reddish tinted fibres which do not reach as far as the root end. (Illustrated in plate 5.)

Magpie tails These are black with a greenish sheen, and are ideal for making the wing-cases of beetles. (Illustrated in plate 5.)

Peacock No doubt the most useful of all. The herls come from the long 'eye' and 'sword' tails, and vary in colour from bright green to deep bronze. The bronze herl is used in many well-known patterns such as the Coachman, Coch-y-Bonddu, Alder, etc. (Illustrated in plate 5.)

The herls on peacock and ostrich are quite bushy, but to use them to the best advantage one must know how to take advantage of their special characteristics. To be a good fly tyer, one must not only know how to tie the materials on to the hook, but also how to work with them to achieve the best results. The natural curve of the fibres on a wing quill, for instance, can be utilised to give a desired curve to the wing being made from them.

The herls used for bodies or butts also have a helpful characteristic in that the fibres on the quills run along one edge only. If a quill is cut across, looking at the two ends produced, one sees the cross-section as illustrated. (Fig. 1.)

Peacock and ostrich herls have this characteristic very markedly, and by taking advantage of this a neat, well-shaped tag can be put on a salmon fly, and a good, full body on a trout fly.

For the butt, the ostrich herl should be tied in underneath the hook shank and on the extreme right of the space devoted to the butt, with the fibres on the left-hand side (Fig. 2). The herl is then wound once to the extreme left, as in Fig. 2, and the remaining turns made to the right, so as to cover this first turn, as Figs. 3 and 4. You will find that this method always produces good results.

For a trout fly body, I always use two strands of peacock herl tied in together at the tail end of the fly, both having the fibres or flue on the left-hand side. The two quills are wound one after the other, each turn of the rearmost quill being brought down on top of the foremost one, as shown in Fig. 5. This produces a much fuller body than if the two quills are twisted together, as is advocated in some fly-tying books.

There is also the problem of how to avoid the gap which often appears between one of these herl bodies and its hackle. The hackle should be tied in at the eye of the hook, and not close up to the body. The tying silk is then wound back to the body,

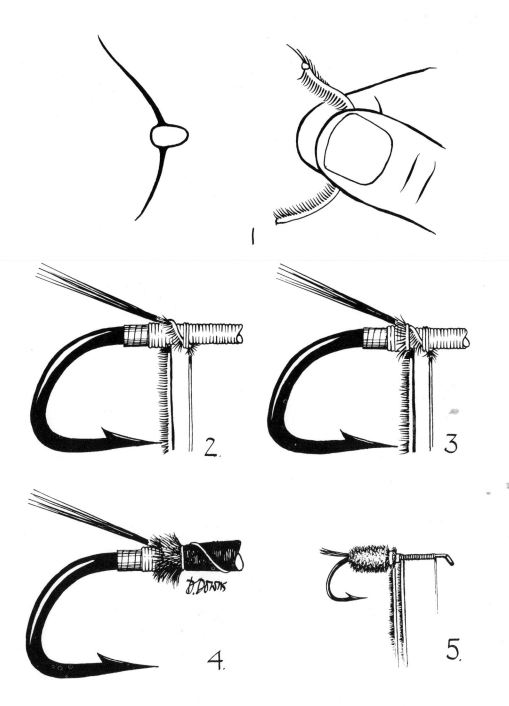

D. DONTK

followed by the hackle, which must be wound right up to the herl body. The tying silk is then wound back to the eye, through the hackle, and tied off. This method eliminates any gap and also ensures a firm fixing of the hackle.

When selecting herls for tags or bodies, it is, of course, necessary to choose those which have plenty of flue on them. This varies considerably, and the selection should be made according to the size of the fly being tied.

Quills

The herls that go to make up the actual bright coloured 'eye' of the peacock tail (Fig. 1) deserve special mention. When stripped of their flue they have a double colour, the part from which the flue is stripped being brown, and the remainder of the quill being beige or grey. The lightness of this colour varies in the quills, and the eyes should be inspected at the back to check that they are light in colour. When wound round the hook shank, such a double-marked quill gives a very life-like imitation of the rib markings of many natural insects, and forms the body material of well-known patterns such as the Red Quill, Blue Upright, Rusty Varient, Ginger Quill, etc. The quills need to be dyed for some of these patterns.

The supply of plain quills is practically limitless as they can be obtained from any quill feathers in the fly tyer's possession. They are pared from the shiny outer face of the quill with a sharp knife, and any pith adhering to the back can be scraped off with a finger nail.

The double-marked quills from the eye tail start at the greenish-yellow triangle at the base of the eye. (Illustrated in plate 5.) All the quills below this point are of one colour only. Quills are very delicate and unless treated with care will break very easily.

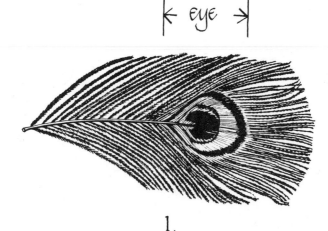

1.

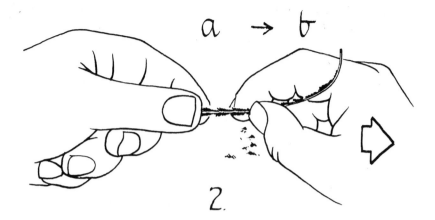

One method of stripping them is as follows: hold the quill in the left forefinger and thumb, leaving about half an inch of the root end projecting to the right. Now scrape it from **a** to **b** between the right thumb nail and the ball of the right forefinger (Fig. 2), and, at intervals, between the right forefinger nail and the ball of the right thumb. This will ensure that both sides of the quill are treated in the same manner. Move the quill to the right a little more, and carry out the same process until about one inch has been cleaned. This will be sufficient for bodies on hooks up to size 12.

Another method which may be found more satisfactory is as follows: place the quill on a small sheet of glass, or any other smooth or glossy surface, and hold it in position with the left forefinger. An old razor blade is now used for the scraping, and the quill must be turned over so that both sides are cleaned. The blade should slope slightly to the right, so that its edge does not bite into the quill and split it (Fig. 3).

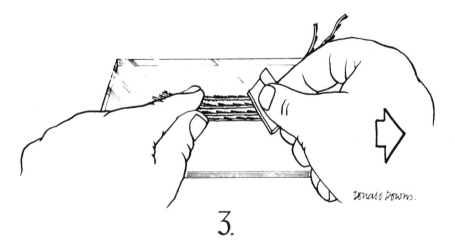

The second method will be found the quicker of the two, although the fingernail may still have to be brought into play for the odd fibre that proves stubborn.

There are always a good many breakages when one starts to strip peacock quills, but they become less as one's experience increases. The thing to remember is not to strip too much at a time, and this applies more to the fingernail method than it does to the razor blade method. More than one quill can be scraped at a time, as shown in Fig. 3.

Another method, and a very good one, is to use a pencil rubber instead of the razor blade. The heavy, soft type of rubber used by artists and draughtsmen is the best, as shown in Fig. 4.

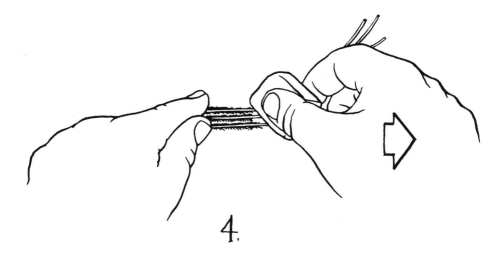

4.

Body materials allow one to use the scope of one's imagination to a far greater extent than do other materials such as wings or hackles, and many new items can be used which are produced for completely different purposes. Sheet PVC is cut into strips and used for such flies as the Polystickle: plastic raffia (or Raffene to give it its trade name) is used for the back of the same pattern and also, because of its wide range of colours, for the backs of many nymphs and beetles. Packaging twines are made in many different plastic materials, including those which simulate a metallic finish (particularly popular at Christmas and other festive occasions), and all these can be used by the imaginative fly dresser. No doubt many more will be made available as the years go by, although I would hesitate to assume that one day man-made fibres will replace the original feathers and furs which have been the basic materials since the earliest days of fly dressing.

One item of body material which should have special mention is Christmas glitter powder, because of the way it is applied. Unlike other body materials it is 'applied' not wound, and the idea was passed to me by Taff Price, author of *Lures for Game, Coarse and Sea Fishing*, and *Rough Stream Trout Flies*.

His instructions were quite simple: form the body out of wool, soak in varnish, then roll in silver or gold Christmas glitter powder and allow to dry before proceeding with the rest of the usual dressing. This gives a scintillating all-flashy body, made up of separate silver or gold scales like the real thing!

However, when Donald Downs came to illustrate the idea in his usual thorough manner, he evolved one or two ideas of his own which are clearly shown in his drawings.

Fig. 1 shows the wool body wound on and Fig. 2 the application of the varnish to the top of the body only. Instead of rolling the fly in a single colour as suggested

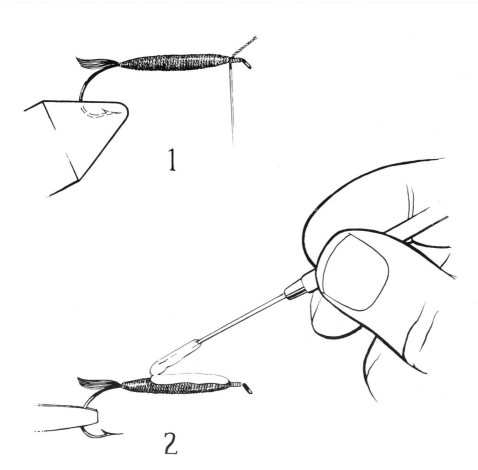

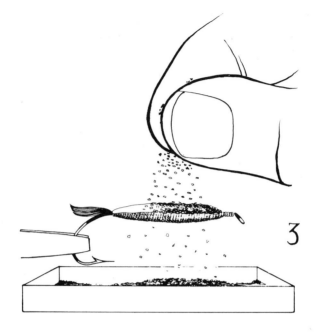

by Taff, Fig. 3 shows the fly being held over the box containing the glitter, which is
then sprinkled on. By turning the fly over and repeating the process with a different
coloured glitter powder, a dual-coloured body can be achieved as shown in Fig. 4.
Fig. 5 shows a fly with the top of one colour and a barred effect along the sides and
underneath.

  The glitter powder can be obtained from any large store or stationery shop, and
the colours available are silver, gold, various reds and blues. It will thus be seen how
many variations of colouring may be achieved by using Donald's method.

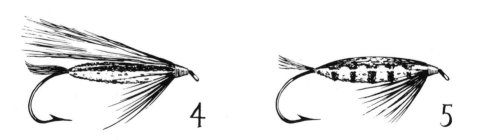

Deer hair for bodies

One material for bodies has made more impact on fly dressing than any other during the 1960s and 1970s – deer body hair. It was first brought to my notice in the early 1950s when I started to get requests for instruction on how to make the head of the Muddler Minnow. Since then, I must have written more about deer hair bodies than any other form of fly-tying procedure, except winging.

The material in question is the body hair of the common red deer, and as the colour varies from a red-brown through grey to pale buff, and finally to white, several colour variations are possible. For instance, using grey, white, grey and so on will produce a barred effect, as will the white dyed in various colours, and grey dyed black.

I have discussed the application of deer hair in many articles and nearly all my books but, because of the unique procedure, I do not think it would come amiss if some of it was repeated here, even though this is not a book of fly-tying instruction.

The reason we have to use the *body* hair of the deer is because of the texture of the hairs. The individual fibres are stiff, hollow and quite thick, and it is these qualities which make possible the particular method of application. The finer hairs, say from the tail, will not spin round the hook shank as will the stiffer and thicker body hairs. The actual method of application is very simple (once it is known), and requires little practice. For the Muddler it is as follows: proceed with the dressing until the stage shown in Fig. 1 (overleaf), where a hair wing has been added, is reached. Leave the front part of the shank bare, as the hair will not spin properly over a silk covering. (The Oak Turkey wing slips are not shown, as these would have interfered with the clarity of the drawings.) Fig. 2 shows the bunch of deer hair fibres placed on top of the hook shank. It is important that they are cut off right at their roots, to give the necessary length of 'ruff'. This illustration also shows the two initial turns of tying silk which are the essential feature of tying in and spinning the deer hair. To ensure that the tips of the hairs are all level, they can be dropped into a pen-holder or lipstick case tip first.

It is now that special attention should be given to this drawing-tight of the silk and spinning of the hair. The usual method is to hold the hair fibres loosely on top of the hook shank until the stage is reached where the silk has to be drawn tight. At this critical moment they are then released to enable the whole bunch to revolve round the hook shank. This, however, results in the short butts becoming mixed up with the long tips in the hackle thus formed, and it is this mixing that should be avoided. Instead of letting the whole bunch go free, the tips are revolved round the shank by the finger and thumb of the left hand as shown in Fig. 3, at the same speed as the butts are revolved when the silk is pulled tight. It helps at this stage of pulling

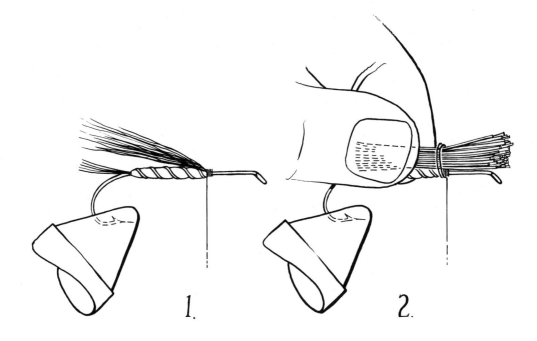

1.

2.

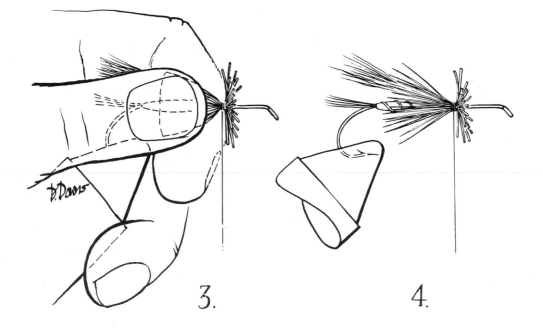

3.

4.

the silk tight if further turns are taken, keeping the silk very tightly pulled all the time. The result should be the ruff shown in Fig. 4, with the first lot of fibres for the head to the right of the tying silk.

Further bunches of hair are now applied without any revolving with the left hand, but instead of cutting them from the skin right at their base, they can be cut about half-way down, or even one-third if the hairs are extra long, and subsequent bunches taken from the lower portion. It is now that the 'packing' method can be used, not forgetting to put the half-hitches or whip finish between each bunch. By this means, two or three times the amount of fibres become available, the resulting amalgam being a mixture of fine tips and thicker bases when spun for the head, as in Fig. 5. This is, of course, the economy aspect of the technique, and also separates head from ruff. The 'packing' method is described later in this chapter.

Next comes the cutting of these fibres to shape the head. Before attacking with the scissors, pull back the ruff with the thumb and first and second fingers of the left hand, and while holding them, push the head fibres to the right with the dubbing needle as shown in Fig. 6. It is now that the advantage of having the shorter hairs for the head can be seen. Once the pushing has achieved a clear distinction between head and ruff, the head can be cut to shape.

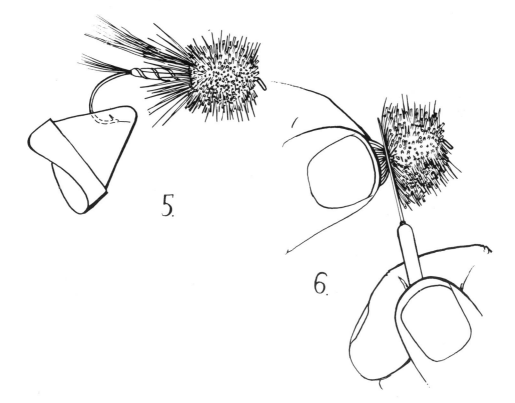

5.

6.

The best way to do this, to achieve a head of uniform thickness round the hook shank, is to make four definite cuts, one each across the top and bottom, and one on each side, the result being as in Fig. 7. Now it is only necessary to round off the corners with more precise and delicate cuts, either as in Figs. 8 and 9, or any other shape desired, such as the flat 'bullhead' effect (true Muddler shape). Spherical or 'tadpole' shapes can also be made by this method.

I would like to emphasise at this juncture that the whole basis of these techniques and their success depends entirely on the amount of pull exerted on the tying silk when revolving the deer hair fibres. This should be the maximum the tying thread will stand, so it is necessary to use something stronger than Gossamer silk, even on the smallest patterns. Nothing weaker than Naples should be used, and I would suggest fine rod-binding silk, about gauge 40, for the larger patterns.

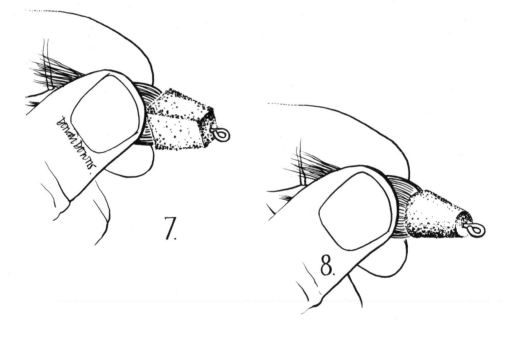

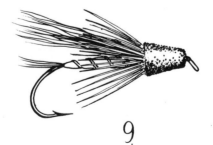

Figs. 1 to 3 of the drawing below show how to cut deer hair from the skin to avoid waste, which is caused by cutting all the hairs used close to the skin and then spinning the lengthy bunch onto the hook shank. With a little forethought, this wastage can be avoided, and the way to go about it is as follows.

When the Muddler is completed up to the point where the head is to be applied, cut the deer hairs off close to the skin as shown at 'L' in Fig. 1. Spin them onto the hook shank in the usual manner, ensuring that the fine tips will point to the rear for the hackle, as required for the dressing as in Fig. 2. However, when this part of the procedure is completed, it is not necessary to use whole lengths of hair to complete the head, so they may be cut off in two sections as shown by 'S' and 'S', also in Fig. 1. These shorter hairs are then added to the hook shank to complete the area required for the head, as shown in Fig. 3, and they are then cut to shape, as shown overleaf on the complete fly in Fig. 4.

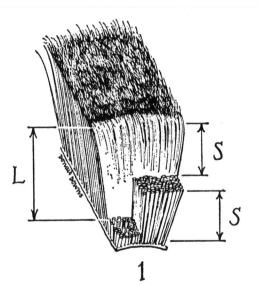

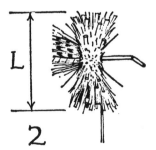

1

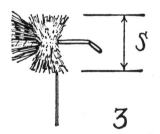

2

3

Some fly tyers do not bother to tie in the body hairs to provide a hackle, so the idea of cutting the hairs off in two separate halves is even more economical for them, doubling the amount they have available for Muddler heads, or any deer hair bodies they may be tying. The best method to ensure uniform thickness of the body or head is to cut off the top half of the hairs first, grip them between two fingers of the left hand while you cut off the base half, and then match the two bunches together into one single bunch, rolling them between the thumb and forefinger to ensure a good mixture of thicknesses.

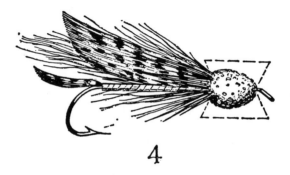

4

Deer hair is now used on many patterns besides the Muddler group, especially as the spun deer hair has very good floating qualities. On one occasion when Donald Downs and myself were attending an exhibition as demonstrators, we were approached by an angler who asked us to make a mayfly with a deer hair body. His request was prompted by our assertions about the floatability of deer hair bodies, and we were very gratified to learn only a week later that he had taken several good chalk-stream trout on the fly tied, and that it proved virtually unsinkable! I can vouch for this from personal experience, and as I always impregnate my flies with a silicone floatant immediately after they are tied (not on the day I go fishing), as far as I am concerned this aspect is assured.

In my opinion, the best flies to imitate when using deer hair for the bodies are those which simulate the hatching fly. The Grey Wulff is an excellent example of this type of fly, and my reason for selecting patterns which represent the fly in this stage of its metamorphosis is the fact that the hair enables the fly to float in or on the surface of the water along the entire length of its body, which is the body position of the hatching fly. Cut finely enough, hair bodies can also be used for spent flies, which of course also lie flat on the surface, but I have chosen the hatching version as it is with this that I have had the best angling results.

There is a method that ensures that the hair, once applied, will be firmly attached, and also packed tightly enough for one to cut it into the many shapes possible once the hair is on. I think this method requires special emphasis, as the packing together of the deer hair, once it is spun on, can be quite an arduous chore, and after half a dozen flies or more the tips of the forefinger and thumb can become quite sore.

To help us do this job quickly and easily without these drawbacks, all we need is a used ball-point pen with its innards and writing point removed as in Fig. 1. If we are using several different sizes of hooks, pens with differing diameters should of course be acquired.

We proceed as follows: put the hook in the vice and tie in the tail, if one is required. Now release the hook and drop it further down into the jaws of the vice to the position shown in Fig. 2. The tail will lie in the gap in the jaws created by the width of the hook and therefore sustain no damage during the rest of the process. There are two reasons why we drop the hook. One is the fact that, if we did not do so, the continued pressure of the pen against the hair could quite easily break the hook at the bend, and the other is that if the hook is so seated that the base of the tail ends exactly within the front of the vice jaws, we can utilise the latter as a 'tamp' against

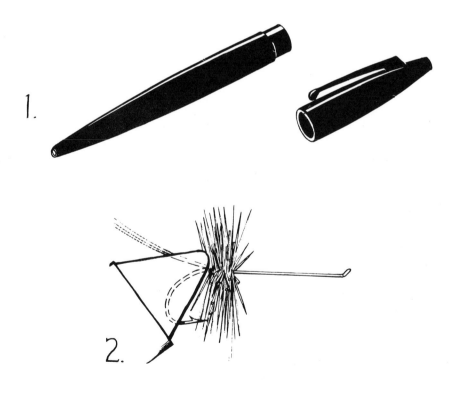

1.

2.

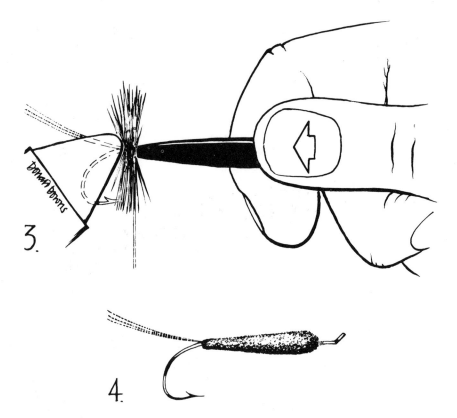

which extra pressure can be exerted when compressing the hairs. This is well
illustrated in Fig. 3.

Fig. 2 also shows the first bunch of deer hairs spun onto the hook shank and
Fig. 3 shows how they are compressed by using the pen barrel.

Fig. 4 shows a body cut to a desired shape, in this instance one suitable for the
hatching or spent flies I mentioned earlier.

Figs. 5–8 are impressions of the various shapes which can be produced when deer
hairs have been well compressed. Please do not take them to be accepted or orthodox
patterns; they are merely an amalgam of suggested uses for deer hair bodies.

Fig. 5 shows a sedge simulation which, with variations, could be adapted for
mayfly types, both hatching and spent. Fig. 6 gives a suggestion of a hatching
nymph, which could be turned into a 'shellback' by using feather fibres or lengths of
deer hair laid over from tail end to front. By leaving a hump at the front to form a
thorax, it could be used as an imitation of nymphs in sizes ranging from mayfly to
the smaller patterns.

Fig. 7 gives a snail shape, and the barred effect is shown to demonstrate how
this can be achieved with close-packed deer hair.

Fig. 8 shows a type of pattern we were once asked to produce for sea-fishing 'flies', and can be used to represent small squid, cuttlefish or any 'nightmare' the tyer cares to think up.

The 'pen-pusher' idea was first shown to us by a member of the Fly-tyers' Round Table (the American equivalent of our Fly Dressers' Guild), and the idea illustrated overleaf in Figs. 9–11 was taken from their magazine. The drawings show how hairs can be lined up by dropping them into the cap of a ball-point pen. Dropping them in root first will of course ensure that they are lined up, but if one drops the tips in first, this has the desired effect also. A simple idea, but one which can save a considerable amount of time.

I know we do not have the same call for them in this country, but our opposite numbers in the USA use the deer hair bodies to produce all sorts of flies and lures

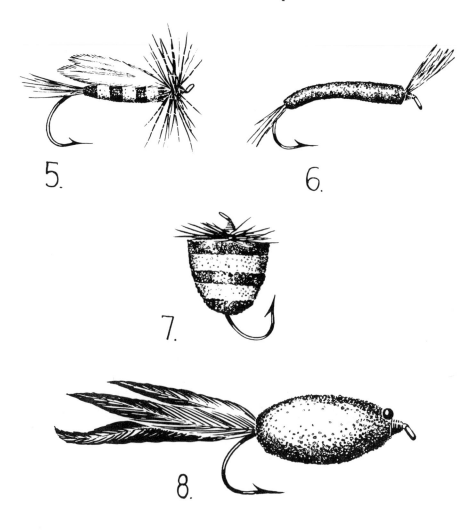

for their angling, mainly because they have a much greater variety of fish to angle for. Their small- and large-mouth bass, for instance, go for frog, crayfish and other imitations for which deer hair is ideally suited. I mention this here merely to illustrate the wide variety of patterns one can tie with a deer hair base to work from.

    These references to the American aspects of fly tying stem from the fact that Donald Downs and myself were invited to the USA as guests of the Fly-tyers' Round Table. The trip was most rewarding and informative in many ways. We spent a weekend in Rhode Island during the run of Blue Fish and 'Stripers', where we were introduced to their form of fly fishing for sea fish. Rhode Island is not very well endowed with fly-fishing water, but so great is the urge in our American cousins to fly fish whenever possible, that they have developed a technique of angling in this manner for sea fish which has to be seen to be really appreciated.

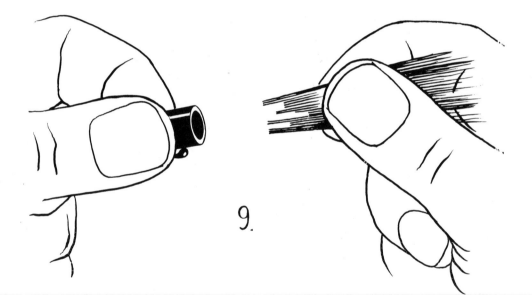

9.

10.

11.

Feathers and furs

left to right (one-third life size)

Peacock sword tail

Wings of Alexandra and Beauly Snow Fly salmon fly

Magpie tail

Wings of beetles, Silver Magpie etc.

Cock pheasant tail

Tail, body and thorax of Pheasant Tail Nymph, wing cases of many nymphs and tails of mayflies

Hen pheasant centre tail

Wings of Invicta and March Brown, and as a substitute for oak turkey for Muddler wings

Peacock eye tail

Herls for bodies of Coachman, Coch-y-Bonddu, Black and Peacock Spider. Quills for quill bodies.

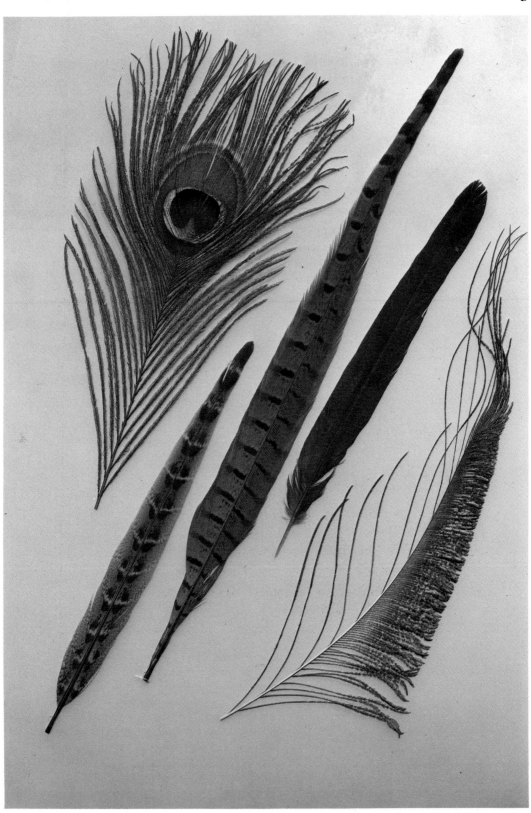

left to right (life-size)

Speckled grouse tail

Wings of Grouse series of flies, such as Grouse and Green, Grouse and Claret etc.

Plain brown partridge tail

Substitute for landrail for wings of sedges and Cow Dung etc.

Speckled partridge tail

Rolled wings of some sedges, wings and tails of March Brown

Waterhen/Moorhen quill

Wings of Early Olive Dun, Leadwing Coachman, large Greenwell's Glory etc.

BOTTOM ROW

Snipe quill

Wings of Dark Bloa, Blue Dun etc.

Starling quill

Wings of Blue Dun, Black Gnat, Olive Quill, Ants, and most grey-winged flies

Substitute cock blackbird quill

Wings of Iron Blue

Substitute hen blackbird quill

Wings of Greenwell's Glory

6

TOP ROW

Grey heron quill

Herl bodies for Kite's Imperial etc., and dyed olive for Rough Olive etc.

Hen pheasant quill

Wings of August Dun, March Brown, Governor, Stone Fly, Caperer etc.

Brown speckled hen quill

Wings of Alder, Dark Sedge etc. May be used as a substitute for brown mallard

Substitute plain brown hen quill (dyed duck)

Wings of sedges, Cinnamon and Gold etc.

BOTTOM ROW

Grey duck quill

Wings of Wickham's Fancy, Blae and Black, and most grey-winged flies. Can be used for small as well as large flies

Blue, white tip wild duck quill

Wings of Butchers, Heckham, Jock etc

Grey teal duck quill

Wings of Wickham's Fancy, Blue Dun etc.

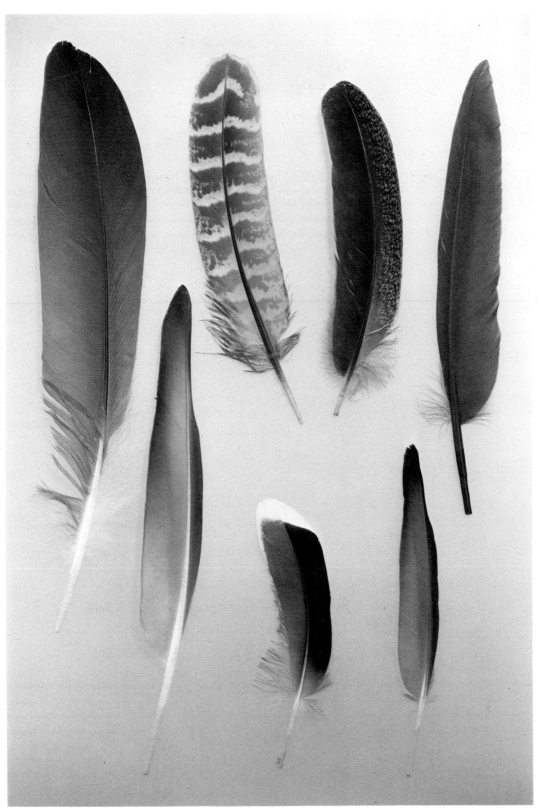

7

Cock hackles – natural

left to right (life-size)

TOP ROW

Ginger (buff), light red game, medium red, dark brown, badger

BOTTOM ROW

Grizzle (Plymouth Rock), cree (coloured grizzle), ginger chinchilla, Greenwell, Coch-y-bonddu

left to right (life-size)

Hen pheasant speckled neck

Hackles for mayflies

Hen pheasant flank

Wings of Matuka

Cock pheasant long brown rump

Hackle of Carey series of flies

Cock pheasant short green rump

Sides of Mrs. Simpson, and bodies of Cordulid, Dragon Fly Nymph etc.

Brown partridge back

Hackle of March Brown, Sam Slick, Game and Green, Partridge and Orange, mayflies etc.

Grey partridge neck

Hackle of Yellow Partridge and mayflies, dyed and undyed

Grouse back

Hackle of Grouse Hackle and some mayflies

Cock pheasant brown neck

Hackle of Bracken Clock etc.

French partridge breast

Hackle of mayflies, natural and dyed

Guinea fowl neck

Hackle of many salmon flies, including Jock Scott, Silver Wilkinson, Butcher etc. Also some mayflies

Substitute blue jay (dyed guinea fowl)

Hackles of Invicta, Thunder and Lightning, Garry, Black Goldfinch etc.

Blue jay

Hackle of Invicta, Thunder and Lightning, Connemara Black etc.

left to right (life-size)

Substitute summer duck round breast (dyed grey mallard)
Wings of Brown Mayfly, fan-winged Cahill etc.

Substitute summer duck flank (dyed grey mallard)
Bunch-wing Cahill, Hendrikson etc.

Grey mallard (wild duck) flank
Wings of Professor etc.

Teal duck flank
Wings of Peter Ross, Teal and Green, Teal Blue and Silver etc.
and sides of many salmon flies

MIDDLE ROW

Golden pheasant red breast
Hackle of Lady Caroline and Shrimp flies

Golden pheasant yellow rump
Hackle of Shrimp flies

Golden pheasant tippet
Tails of sea-trout and lake-trout flies, Peter Ross etc. Wings of
Durham Ranger

Golden pheasant crest (topping)
Tails of Invicta, Golden Olive, and many other lake, sea-trout
and salmon flies. Also used as the topping feather over numerous
salmon fly wings

BOTTOM ROW

Brown mallard (wild duck) shoulder
Wings of Maliard and Claret, Connemara Black, Fiery Brown
etc,. and of numerous salmon flies and lures

Blue peacock neck
Wings of Hen Blue etc.

Hen mallard (wild duck) shoulder
Body and thorax of Cordulid

Substitute ibis (dyed goose)
Tail of Butcher, Hen Blue, Parmachene Belle etc.

Grey squirrel tail and natural cree hackle cape

12

Dyed hackle cape and dyed goose feather

(left) Deer hair *(right)* Dyed bucktail

Detached bodies

The making of detached bodies has always intrigued fly dressers, and the methods used have been most ingenious in many instances. However, the advent of the 'Fly Body' hook has solved this problem to a large extent, but there is one other man-made item I must mention. It is the plastic mayfly body. It is most realistic in appearance and in quantity looks like a heap of maggots. Tails can be added, and the tips sealed again with varnish, and providing the tyer ensures that the hollow bodies are air-tight, they will keep afloat indefinitely. Any pattern of mayfly can be represented, as the bodies are in three shades – cream, pale green olive, and pale brown olive – and are particularly effective for spent patterns. Furthermore, much smaller hooks can be used, such as a No. 14 or 12 standard size, as the detached body eliminates the need for a long-shanked hook with its extra weight.

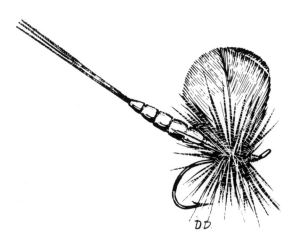

8

Materials for tails

Tail materials create less of a problem than most other items in the fly dresser's collection; in fact, I am prepared to say that the scope is almost limitless.

In the first instance, the most used of all items is the hackle, or rather fibres from it, and as we all gradually accumulate more large hackles than we can ever possibly use, tail fibres are always readily to hand.

However, some hackles make better tails than others, so we still have to use a certain amount of selectivity. For dry flies, spade hackles, or those running up the edge of a cape, provide the stiffest barbules, whereas for wet flies, especially nymphs, the softer, or large, cock hackles, or hen hackles are best. A bunch of stiffish cock hackle fibres, cut short, make a tail for Terry's Terror or the Treacle Parkin of incredible stiffness, as, like the beard on a man's face, the stubble is always much stiffer than a full growth.

For the rather wide tails found on some nymphs, two or three whole hackle tips can be used to good effect.

On some flies, the same feather fibres can be used for both the wing and the tail. The Alexandra is a good example of this, and so is the Parmachene Belle.

Other feathers we can use for many patterns are listed below, but it is only a short list. None of the items present any collecting difficulty.

Cock pheasant centre tails The long fibres on these makes excellent tails, as they have very small hairs along each fibre. This makes the tips extremely suitable for nymphs, and their good length has always made them a popular tail material for mayflies. (Illustrated in plate 5.)

Golden pheasant crest feathers These are used on literally hundreds of fly patterns. A whole feather is used, tied in curving upwards to meet the tip of the wing in most instances. An example of this feather is illustrated in plate 10.

Golden pheasant tippet feathers In the same category as the crest feathers, but bunches of fibres are used, not the whole feather. Also illustrated in plate 10.

Guinea fowl plain blue neck feathers Like the cock pheasant tails, fibres from these feathers have small hairs protruding from them, making them ideal for nymph tails also. They are a smoky blue/grey in colour. There is also a white variety which can be dyed for the olives etc., but I regret to say that they are not very readily available. However, good thick hen hackle fibres make a very good substitute.

Ibis (substitute) This is another feather which provides tail fibres for many patterns, the best known being the Butcher. Feathers from the ibis are of course on the 'unobtainable' list, as it is a protected species. However, almost any stiffish, white feather dyed the correct colour can be used as a substitute, and an example (goose) is also illustrated in plate 10.

Over and above those listed here, one can make use of innumerable feathers as suppliers of tail fibres, including those which are usually kept for wings. Brown mallard and teal flank and breast feathers, grey mallard flank, hen and cock pheasant body feathers, the red or yellow feathers of the cock golden pheasant, partridge tail and body feathers and woodcock body feathers are some examples – in fact, as I said at the beginning, the supply is limitless.

One or two patterns need wool or silk tails, but once again there should be no problem. The floss silks we accumulate for bodies supply the one, whilst any wool shop or tackle shop can supply the other.

In addition to the feathers we use for tails, some of the hairs kept for wings can also be used. Moose mane is good for dry flies and mayflies, being more buoyant and robust than cock pheasant tail fibres, as also are the face whiskers from a hare or rabbit mask. The tips of bucktail hairs will also give a good range of tail fibres.

9
Materials for wings

I think one can state categorically that the wings of all our flies are made from either feather fibre or hair. One or two attempts have been made to produce wings made from nylon fibres, and once there was even a machine for stamping out veined wings that were exact simulations of those found on many natural insects. However, the old axiom, 'If you want to imitate nature – use nature' still holds good, and I know of nothing better than feather or hair to give 'life' or naturalness to our imitations.

Most trout fly wings, especially those used on patterns that are imitations of the natural fly, are made from the wing and tail feathers of various birds. Other patterns, of course, use entirely different materials from different parts of the same birds. This can cause a certain amount of confusion. For instance, the teal supplies us with wing quills for winging (grey), and also the black and white barred flank feathers for winging such flies as the Peter Ross, Teal and Green, etc.

The same applies to the feathers from the mallard duck, whose wings supply us with feathers for the wings of many patterns of flies, and whose brown speckled shoulder feathers are used for the wings of the Mallard series of patterns.

One or two of the feathers required for some patterns are not plentiful, but a substitute can usually be obtained.

Wing quills

Both secondaries and primaries (illustrated in plate 7) are used for winging. In many instances these are the same colour, but in others the secondaries are an entirely different colour from the primaries. The teal and mallard wings are excellent examples of this. They both have grey primaries, but in the case of the teal the secondaries are a shiny green, and the mallard's are a shiny blue.

Before going on to describe the various quills, I think it would be a good idea if I were to explain how best to extract the quills from the wing.

In most cases, it is far cheaper to buy the whole wing if one wants quill feathers for winging purposes, but unless one extracts them with a certain amount of circumspection, the important feather fibres on the quills can be damaged enough to make them unusable.

All wings sold for fly tying should be well dried first, not only for the purpose under discussion, but also because this ensures that they are free from parasites. This drying is carried out by subjecting the wings to a high temperature for several days, so that the fleshy part becomes quite hard and crisp. This process should not be confused with 'cooking' over a short period, which would make the flesh messy and be harmful to the feather fibres.

To extract the quills from the whole wings, I use the following method, which is less harmful to the individual quills than pulling them direct from the flesh.

Grasp the extreme edges of the wing, as in Fig. 1.

Give a sharp tug outwards in both directions, so that the wing separates at the base, as in Fig. 2.

Now take a pair of scissors and cut across the extreme base of the quills on either side, as in Fig. 3 on page 56.

This will result in all the quills parting cleanly and evenly (Fig. 4), and they should then be stored in cellophane envelopes until needed. If you put all the quills from the same pair of wings in the same envelope, exact pairing will be easy.

Some wings, such as mallard, have different coloured quills, so in this case the blue coverts would be stored in one envelope and the grey primaries in another.

Some wings also supply hackles, so these should be stripped off before the cutting process. These include such types as moorhen (under-wing feathers used for

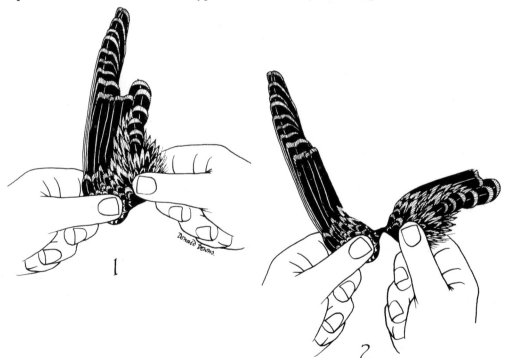

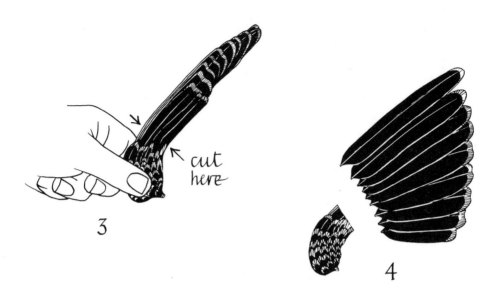

Waterhen Bloa), grouse and woodcock wing front feathers (used for many wet-fly patterns and spider types), and also another feather from the mallard wings – the under-wing white 'satins' (used for wet Coachman).

I would like to emphasise at this point that many of the feathers listed here are now on the protected list, but must be included as they are mentioned in so many dressings. In most instances, a suitable substitute can be found from some available species.

Blackbird The hen bird is lighter in colour than the cock, and its wings supply the materials for Greenwell's Glory. The darker cock's wing feathers are used for the Iron Blue. Of course, the blackbird is now protected, but starling wings dyed the correct colour make ideal substitutes. (Illustrated in plate 6.)

Capercailzie The secondaries and coverts of these wings provide a speckled feather for the wings of alders. They are not very plentiful, however, and the best substitute is the speckled hen wing, which comes from the game hen.

Coot A smoky-blue quill feather suitable for Blue Winged Olive, Blue Dun, etc.

Crow Shiny black, suitable for the Butcher and Watson's Fancy.

Duck, white Used for the wings of the Coachman and Parmachene Belle and, when dyed, they can be used for the wings of sea-trout flies such as The King and The Queen. The fibres 'marry' well very, so that various colours can be mixed for the wings of small salmon and sea-trout flies. The Parson is a good example of the latter.

Duck, wild (mallard) The grey primaries are used for several popular patterns needing a wing of that colour, the Wickham being perhaps the best known. If only two or three fibres are used, they can be incorporated in fairly small patterns, but usually they form the wings of the larger patterns of wet flies. They are used a great deal in America and New Zealand on large wet flies, many of which are based on the patterns used in this country. I have seen them used as the wing material for a Greenwell tied on a No. 8 hook. (Illustrated in plate 7.)

Goose, white The quills are similar to those of the white duck, but much larger. They are suitable for making wings of bass flies and flies for sea fishing.

Grouse The secondaries, if well marked, are used for the Grouse series of flies (Grouse and Claret, etc.), but the tail feather from this bird is generally considered better for this purpose, as it has more pronounced markings and pairs of wings can be obtained from single tails. This is clearly illustrated in plate 6.

Hen, plain (Buff Orpington, Rhode Island Red, etc.) Used for the rolled wings of sedges, and for Autumn Dun and Welshman's Button. They vary in colour from a pale buff to a deep red-brown, and some of the intermediate shades are a suitable substitute for landrail. (Illustrated in plate 7.)

Hen, speckled game These quills are the ones most used for the wings of the alder and also for some of the darker patterns of sedges. The lighter shades can be used as a substitute for grouse tail and wing feathers when tying the Grouse series of flies (Grouse and Green, etc.). (Illustrated in plate 7.)

Jay The blue coverts from these wings have alternate light and dark blue bars, and although they are used primarily as hackles for sea-trout and salmon flies, just the tips of the feathers are also used for wings in one or two patterns. The larger primaries are used for winging also, the Saltoun and the Hawthorn being two of the patterns on which they are found.

Mavis thrush A pinkish-brown feather, sometimes used for Greenwell's Glory and also as a substitute for landrail, which is now rare.

Owl, tawny and barn These are used when tying moths, and also for the wings of the Brown Owl and Cinnamon.

Partridge Used for the wings of the Grannom and also on very small patterns that would normally call for a cock or hen pheasant wing.

Pheasant, cock For the Artful Dodger and Nobbler, etc.

Pheasant, hen Both secondaries and primaries are used, and supply the wings for many popular patterns: March Brown, Caperer, August Dun, Governor, etc. (Illustrated in plate 7.)

Plover (Lapwing) Not an extremely popular winging material but sometimes used for the Iron Blue and Butcher.

Rook Similar to the crow, but smaller, and also suitable for the Butcher and Watson's Fancy.

Snipe For the Blue Dun, Seth Green, etc. and in fact for numerous flies that call for a grey wing. (Illustrated in plate 6.)

Starling This is, without doubt, the most useful of all the wings. Both secondaries and primaries can be used, and they provide the wings for all duns and olives, and many other patterns, such as the Hare's Ear and Ginger Quill variants. In fact, any pattern that calls for a grey wing. (Illustrated in plate 6.)

Teal As previously mentioned, the primaries and secondaries differ in colour. The grey primaries can be used as are those from the snipe or starling, but as they are coarser in texture they are only used on larger sizes of the same patterns. (Illustrated in plate 7.) The secondaries have a bright green sheen on them and are used for sea- and lake-trout patterns. The Delius is one of these.

Waterhen (Moorhen) The quills are brownish-grey, suitable for the Olive Dun and other patterns that call for a dun-coloured wing. (Illustrated in plate 6.)

Woodcock These quills supply the wings for the Woodcock series of flies (Woodcock and Green, etc.), and also for Hardies Favourite, Gravelbed and Mole.

Tail feathers for wings

Tail feathers, with the exception of grouse, are not as popular for winging as wing quills. The reason for this is that the fibres on the tails do not stay together as well as those on the wing quills. For large patterns, however, it is sometimes necessary to use the tails as the fibres on these are much longer. A good instance of this is the March Brown. Hen pheasant tail is almost invariably used on the larger patterns of this fly.

Speckled partridge tail feathers Used for the wings of sedges, and for the whisks of the March Brown. (Illustrated in plate 6.)

Plain brown partridge tail feathers Substitute for landrail wing, for the Cow-Dung, etc. (Illustrated in plate 6.)

Hen pheasant tail feathers For the wings of the Invicta and the larger patterns of the March Brown. (Illustrated in plate 5.)

Speckled grouse tail feathers The best feather to use when winging the Grouse series of flies – Grouse and Claret, etc. (Illustrated in plate 6.)

White tip turkey rump feathers These are used for fairly large flies that require a feather with a white tip, such as the McGinty.

Magpie tails A feather with a rich dark green sheen, which is used for the wings of the Magpie and Silver, and makes an ideal material for the wing cases of beetles.

Hackle wings

Using hackles for wings introduces a wide range of possibilities. The tips can be utilised for spinners and spent flies, or the hackle can be wound in the usual fashion and then all the fibres 'bunched' above the hook shank for upright wings, or in two equal halves at right-angles to the shank for spent flies. Used in this way they make very durable and attractive wings.

A single hackle tip, usually from a bright spade hackle, can be used when tying one of the down-winged types of fly such as a sedge.

Hackles for wings are most popular on streamer flies, one of which is illustrated here.

This type of fly was in common use in America long before it became a popular 'everyday' fly here. Admittedly, hackle-winged lures called 'terrors' were in use in this country, but only for sea-trout in our river estuaries. Now, however, there must be few reservoir fishermen who do not have examples of streamers in their fly boxes.

The middle and large feathers on a cape are ideal for streamers, but so also are long saddle hackles, and although they are not really hackles in the true sense, body feathers such as hen pheasant flank are used, mainly for the Matuka type of fly originating in New Zealand. This feather is illustrated in plate 9.

Hair wings

The use of hair instead of feather fibre for the wings of flies has become increasingly popular, especially during the 1960s and 1970s in Great Britain. It has always been a popular material in North America and Canada, a natural consequence of the prolific animal life on that continent. The Indians used it on lures long before the white man came, and many flies have names with Indian connotations. Hair is used mainly on 'bucktail' flies, and this has become a name in common usage although not every fly is tied with bucktail hairs.

The reason for the increasing popularity of such flies in this country is mainly the success of hair-winged flies on the many new reservoirs, although my company first started to stock the various types when hair began to take over from feathers on the salmon fly. We do not have the proliferation of types in Great Britain that are found in North America, which is understandable, as I stated earlier, but the range available is sufficient for our needs, especially as hair can usually be dyed quite easily. Our list consists of the following types: squirrel (common grey, brown, brown-barred and black), calf tails, white and dyed any colour, and bucktails (imported from America) which are available in white, brown or dyed colours (see plate 14). Other types are badger hair, marten tails, deer body hair, stoat tails, moose mane, and also mohair.

For anyone wishing to match up a particular hair, or trying to make a new design, the following descriptions of the various tails will no doubt be useful.

Squirrel tails (a squirrel tail is illustrated in plate 11).
Grey These are barred brown/olive at the base, grey in the centre, and finish with white points. The fibres of the tail nearest to the body are best for small flies, and those at the tip sometimes have a length of over $1\frac{1}{2}$ in. for larger flies. The blue under-fur can be used for dubbing, and these tails can be dyed any colour. Very useful for lures and hair-winged salmon flies.
Black These tails are usually quite large, often with a working length of 2 in. and over. They are greyish at the base, darkening to black, glossy tips. A fine strong hair for black-winged lures.
Parey This is a small tail, but the hairs at the tip are quite long. The hairs are marked (from the base through to their tips) dark grey – light grey – dark tan – tan – ginger and very dark brown tips. It is an ideal hair for salmon flies, tube flies, and the usual substitute for brown mallard in hair-winged flies.
Red/Brown These vary in shade from light red-brown to dark, and the darker ones also make a good substitute for bronze (brown) mallard feathers.

Dark Brown A very dark brown, almost black.

Canadian Fox Squirrel A ginger shade, with a black bar nearer to the tips than the base.

Dovre Brown A barred grey base, shading to dark brown, and another ideal substitute for dressings which normally use brown mallard feathers.

Bucktails These are deer tails, and the underpart is white, with the top side varying from greyish brown to dark brown. A very good hair for large lures and salmon flies (also sea flies). They also dye well, the white part supplying direct colours, and the dark side producing some interesting shades.

Calf tails The hair length on these varies considerably, being quite short where the tail joins the body, but of a good length at the tip. Most of the tail is white, it dyes well, and is a good substitute for bucktail, especially on small flies or where a fine, crinkly hair is required.

Badger hair A good hair when straight uncrinkled wings are desired. The colour range from the root is cream, tan, black, white. It is the same hair as is used for good-quality shaving brushes, if this helps the description.

Stoat tail A very dark hair, almost black, and the correct material for the Stoat Tail fly. Quite short in length, the longest hairs are sometimes a little sparse. If a large Stoat Tail fly or tube fly is required, dark brown squirrel or dovre squirrel can be used.

Marten tails A brown, softish hair with good long fibres.

Goat hair A good, long hair of 4–5 in. but rather soft.

Moose mane Long fibres, but stiffish. Coloration, off-white to brown at the tips.

Breast and flank feathers

These feathers are used mainly for winging sea- and lake-trout flies. They are rather more difficult to handle than quill or tail feathers, being of a much softer texture. This difficulty, however, can be overcome with practice. They are used in exactly the same manner, in that left and right feathers are used for left and right wings.

Brown (or bronze) mallard shoulder feathers These form the wings of many well-known patterns of flies, especially the Mallard series, such as the Mallard and Claret. Other patterns are Connemara Black, Fiery Brown, Golden Olive, Black and Orange, etc. (Illustrated in plate 10.)

Teal flank feathers This is a black and white barred feather and is also used mainly for lake- and sea-trout flies. Perhaps the best known of these is the Peter Ross, an illustration of which, with the feather itself, is given on page 62. Other well-known patterns using the teal flank wings are the Teal series, such as the Teal and Green, Teal and Claret, Teal Blue and Silver, Parson, etc. In many patterns a few fibres are used as 'cheeks' on some other wing feather, the Don being one of these. (Illustrated in plate 10.)

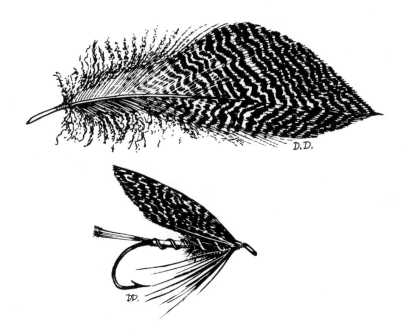

Grey mallard (drake) breast and flank feathers These feathers are used similarly to the brown mallard and teal feathers, but they are more popular in America than in the United Kingdom. Some of the American patterns are the Rube Wood, Laramie, Grizzly King, Queen of Waters and Professor. Well-known English patterns are the John Spencer and John Storey. They are also used for the wings of mayflies, dyed and undyed. (Illustrated in plate 10.)

Summer duck flank feather, or substitute This is very similar to brown mallard but lighter in colour. It is also more popular in America than in the United Kingdom, mainly because it is indigenous to that country. The best-known fly that uses this feather for its wings is the Cahill, a pattern that is almost synonymous with fly fishing in America. Others are the Hoskins and the Gordon. It is also used on many dry flies. The fibres are tied in 'bunch' fashion as it is termed in America. We use a similar type in this country on our hackle-fibre wings. (Illustrated in plate 10.)

Mandarin duck flank feathers The feathers from the mandarin duck are almost an exact duplicate of those of the summer duck. Consequently, they can be used as substitutes when summer duck feathers are hard to get. The fibres are a little 'stringier', so do not stay 'married' quite as well as those of the summer duck, but this can be an asset when 'bunch' wings are being tied.

Summer duck and mandarin duck white breast feathers These are round spade-shaped feathers, and their natural contour makes them ideal for 'fan' wings.

Widgeon shoulder feathers These are grey speckled feathers, ideally suited for sea- and lake-trout flies such as the Teal Blue and Silver, Peter Ross, etc. They are more distinctively marked than grey mallard flank feathers, but not as heavily barred as teal flank. Their fibres stay together better than do those of most wildfowl body feathers, and consequently they are much easier to tie in.

Herl wings

There are not many patterns of flies that use separate herls for wings, but the one that comes to mind immediately is the Alexandra. For this the herls from the green peacock sword tails are used. (Illustrated in plate 5.)

Another pattern is the Ilen Blue, which uses herls from the blue neck feathers of the peacock.

Whole feather wings

This type of wing is usually tied with the extreme tip of a whole feather, or two of them back to back. The most used are:

Blue kingfisher feathers These are the electric blue feathers from the body of the kingfisher. Two of them, back to back, form the wings of the Blue Kingfisher.

Blue jay feathers These are the dark and light blue barred coverts, and are also used back to back.

Jungle cock feathers These feathers come from the cape of the jungle cock, and are in fact its hackles. They are unique, as each one has a white or cream 'eye' which appears to have been enamelled on. Two of these, back to back, form the wings of the Demon and Jungle Cock flies. They are also used as cheeks or shoulders on many patterns such as Watson's Fancy, Jungle Alexandra, and many hair-wing and streamer flies. However, they are now on the protected list, and we have to resort to substitutes. The best of these is an ordinary black hen's hackle which has the 'eyes' painted on with polyurethane paint of suitable colour.

Some years ago, in writing about the choice of hackle, I referred to our modern domestic chicken as being derived from the Red Jungle Fowl (*Gallus gallus*) with help from the other three jungle fowl, the Ceylon (*G. Lafayettii*), the Green (*G. varius*) and the Grey or Sonnerats (*G. sonnerati*). I was taken to task for suggesting that the latter has any part in the modern chicken, as there is apparently no evidence to suggest it – to which I am bound to reply, 'What a pity,' as it would be a marvellous thing for fly tyers if the Sonnerati Jungle Fowl were as easy to breed from as a chicken.

Due to the demand that fly tyers created for the neck feathers of this bird, it was in danger of extinction. Realising this danger, the Indian Government barred any export of the skins or capes in 1967, but, in spite of this, many capes continued to come into England as it was then perfectly legal to import them. This has been stopped, as the British Government made it illegal to import the capes or skins, so the ban was then imposed from both directions! In spite of this, the Sonnerati Jungle Fowl, which is confined to western and southern India, up to Mount Abu in the north-west and east to the Godevari River, and in Central India and Rajputara, has continued to decline and efforts are being made to reintroduce it through hand-reared birds to areas from which it died out.

The upshot is that we cannot expect to see capes as freely available in the years to come. However, for many years now the Sonnerati Jungle Fowl has been kept in this country by a few enthusiasts specialising in the keeping and breeding of rare pheasants, to which family all the jungle fowl belong. As a result, there is a small stock of these unique birds in this country. I have talked to one such collector, Mr Keith Howman, who told me something of the ways of keeping these birds and breeding from them.

He started with a pair of Sonnerati and in two years built up a small flock of twelve birds. Although not in any way related to the domestic chicken, many of their behaviour characteristics are similar. For instance, unlike most members of the pheasant family, they will live very happily as a flock. The dominant cock bird, as with chickens, will from time to time assert himself, but fights are seldom serious, unlike most of those involving pheasants which are usually fatal.

Sonnerati will feed on the same food as a chicken and like to scratch the ground in the same way. However, being a smallish, lightly-built bird, they do not ruin grass as chickens do. Their principal diet is turkey or game pellets mixed in winter with some wheat. They also like some green food such as lettuce.

One important point on which they differ from chickens is in hardiness. They do not like extremes of cold and wet and need a good warm shelter if they are to winter well and lay well for the following spring. They do not need any additional heat but they must be able to roost out of the wind and wet.

Although shaped rather like a bantam, the Sonnerati Jungle Fowl is a very proficient flier and when frightened will fly up to the nearest perch, uttering a harsh cackling cry. They need, therefore, to be kept in pens that are completely roofed in with netting.

Compared with most members of the pheasant family, the Sonnerati are not very prolific layers, but their eggs do, on the other hand, appear to hatch well in incubators, which is a big advantage as suitable broodies are not always available at the right moment. The chicks are strong and easy to rear using the usual turkey or pheasant chick starter crumbs. If possible, they should also be given some green food such as chickweed, which all pheasant chicks like. The chicks are easily reared under a brooder lamp.

The cock birds do not fully colour up until their second year – however, the valuable neck feathers do grow to a limited extent on the young cock birds and as they are all small feathers they are well worth trying to collect during the moult.

In addition to the Sonnerati Jungle Fowl, Mr Howman also keeps the Red Jungle Fowl, of which there are only a very few pure-bred birds in this country.

It is perhaps time that fishermen began to replace some of what they have (most inadvertently) destroyed, and I hope a few more enthusiasts may be encouraged to try and keep these interesting birds, and perhaps some of the other rare pheasants that also contribute valuable feathers for the fly tyer.

A jungle cock
feather

Marabou plumes These are long, fluffy feathers obtained from the turkey, and they have become increasingly popular as a wing material in the U.K. during the 1970s. Once again, we have adopted and adapted dressings from the U.S.A. and Canada, and many marabou patterns are now creeping into the lists of British flies. They look something like ostrich herls, but are much softer, and their popularity stems from their lifelike action in water. Being white originally, it is possible to dye them any colour.

IO

Hackles for fly tying

There is no doubt that the most used, and therefore the most necessary, item of fly-tying material is the hackle, be it from common poultry (not so common in many instances), or from the plumage of some other bird. The latter presents no problems, but unfortunately the number of hackles available from poultry is never sufficient to meet the demand. This may seem strange when one considers it is estimated that the chicken is the only species of bird with a total population larger than that of man – and that this estimate puts the poultry population at 3000 million. Added to this is the fact that the chicken is also one of the most widespread birds, being found practically anywhere where man has penetrated.

Neck Hackles

Spade Hackles

Spey Hackles

Saddle Hackles

Be this as it may, the difficulties preventing the reaping of this fantastic harvest are manifold, and include ensuring that the birds are killed only when the plumage is at its best, curing of the skins, storage so that they are protected from parasites and, of course, collection. These problems can only be overcome if the processes are carried out within the scope of large commercial organisations which breed poultry for the table, and although this is done, and in fact many thousands of hackles do reach the fly tyer in this way, they represent but a miniscule proportion of the total poultry population.

In subsequent parts of this chapter I deal with some of these factors, and also show how individual fly tyers may overcome the shortages of necessary types of hackles. I consider, however, that it would be of interest if everyone knew the history of this bird, whose plumage is vital to our craft, and its evolution during the many centuries to the 'general provider' familiar to us all at the present time.

History of the hackle

Because of its long usefulness to man, the history of the chicken is lost in antiquity, but it is generally accepted that it is descended from the Red Jungle Fowl, *Gallus gallus*, with some help from two other species of *Gallus* which also stem from south-eastern Asia. They are *G. lafayettii*, the Ceylon Jungle Fowl, and *G. varius*, the Green Jungle Fowl. Because of this mixed ancestry, some scientists refer to our modern chicken as *G. domesticus*. The actual time of the jungle fowl's domesticity is, as I have said, lost in antiquity, but there are Asiatic records of it which go back 3000 years.

The earliest civilisations known to have domesticated the Red Jungle Fowl are those of the Indus Valley in India, and excavations in the cities of Mohenjo-Daro and Harappa, which flourished around 2500 B.C. have disclosed evidence of the presence of domestic fowl. It is also thought that even in those ancient times the birds were bred to increase their size for the table.

By the time we get to 500 B.C., chickens were part of the scene in most civilised countries such as Japan, Greece and Italy, and in the rest of western Europe by the first century B.C. This, of course, was due to the spread of the Roman Empire.

During its evolution, the chicken was venerated for its 'sacred' ability to foretell the future, and it became the national symbol of France, at the time it was known as Gaul, mainly for its strength, pride and fighting ability. In fact, it is (or was) this latter ability which resulted in the word 'game' being added to the species, recorded historically in this country in the name of 'Old English Game', a breed very closely associated with its early ancestor (the Red Jungle Fowl), and also with the so-called 'sport' of cock-fighting.

Eventually, of course, these 'game' attributes of the bird became secondary to its culinary value, and although this has resulted in a vast increase in the numbers of birds produced, it also meant a reduction of the quality of the feathers needed by the fly tyer. Put simply, the closer the bird to its original wild ancestors, the better the quality of the hackle, but this quality declines in the same ratio to the amount of time a particular strain has been kept in captivity for domestic purposes – the ultimate being those birds reared in batteries as 'broilers', whose plumage is useless for our purposes.

Therefore, if wild birds produce the best plumage, the next group down which can produce suitable hackles for us is birds closely associated with their wild ancestors, which also live an 'open range' existence. The nearest we can get are the Asiatic birds which continue to live this open range existence, and which are bred from strains not over-long domesticated.

Fortunately for us, climatic conditions in these areas enable the birds to be bred not only for culinary purposes, but also facilitate the saving of the plumage on the skin without the necessity of building large and expensive curing establishments. This means that the hackles can be removed as 'capes' from the birds, stretched and dried under natural conditions, and made available in this form to the fly tyer.

It is thought that the first Old English Game came from the crossing of a black rooster with a white hen, which resulted in the many types of hackles which have a black centre, such as those used for Grey Duster, Greenwell's Glory and Coch-y-Bonddu, to name only the best known. These were the result of crossing the O.E.G. with Red Game, Rhode Island Red, Buff Orpington, and many other strains which have evolved since the domestication of the Asiatic birds. The degree to which interbreeding has produced such a great variety of colours and permutations of colours is described later in this chapter, as are my methods for reproducing these colours and types when the originals are not available. Interbreeding with many other strains produced the honeys, honey duns, blue duns and duns – all well-known fly-tyers' shades.

The breeding of Old English Game fowl

Good quality hackles for fly making are always in short supply, mainly because of increasing demand. Hackles for dry flies in particular fall into this category, and the position would be even worse if it were not for the fact that we can use dyed substitutes for colours such as those which come from the Old English Game fowl. Even these substitutes can never replace the more subtle shades in the natural hackles, particularly the honey shades, which may have dun flecks in them, or the dun shades with honey flecks. I see a cape like this about once a year, in spite of the many thousands which pass through our warehouse, and a really first-class cape of the dun or blue dun variety is more of a once-every-five-years event.

Even as long ago as 1892 it was found necessary to make an attempt to revive interest in the types of fowl required by anglers, and this was done at the Fish Exhibition held at the Royal Aquarium, Westminster. An earlier attempt had been made at the Crystal Palace Poultry Show in November 1871, when a prize was given for 'Fowls with plumage suitable for fly fishing'. To this, however, there was but a poor response, only four pens being exhibited, and the Rev. H. I. Stokes, of Grindon Rectory, Leek, Staffordshire, taking first and second prizes with the Blue Dun. These were the old style of 'pit' game birds, strongly made and with hard feathers. This texture, with the colouring, was just what was wanted; the hackles were short and firm, and the mid-rib and quill of the feathers dun, as also was the underside. They did not go limp in water, as did the softer Andalusian, and even in those times it was said, 'The blue-breasted blue and the blue-breasted dun Game have gradually become scarce, and it is difficult to find any of the true, strong made, old breed asure-fronted with the dark blue hackle.'

The prizes offered at the 1892 Exhibition were quite substantial and numerous, the proprietors of the *Fishing Gazette* heading the list with a liberal donation, and the judges being Captain Lampert of Canterbury and Mr Harrison Weir, FRHS, author of *Our Poultry*, 1902.

The beautiful, bright, Old English blue-breasted blue Game was largely used to stiffen the make and add lustre to the colour of the Andalusian (it is a mistakenly held view that the best Blue Duns are 'Andalusians'), so many of this cross were sent to the Exhibition in the hope of winning. In the hens, absolutely pure Andalusians were considered good enough, their white, deaf ears or ear-lobes unmistakably testifying to their ancestry. Although there were only three or four Blue Dun or Dun cocks that were considered above average, they were the redeeming feature of this part of the show, plus a few others of quality which also had useful colours.

Prizes were also given for the best cards of hackle pluckings, which consisted of small bunches of hackles of various colours – all from Game birds, of course. Some of the colours described are quite mouth-watering, and I can do no better than quote Harrison Weir, who said, 'Some [were] particularly vivid, while others were of a tone and texture so dearly loved, desired and coveted, which proved to be an art study in themselves, so rare and beautiful were the tints, though so lovely are the delicate colours and blendings, that neither words nor even drawings can give but a faint idea of their actuality.' I am sure a description of some of them would interest those readers who may have little or no idea of what was available at one time: Hazel, a beautiful grey-toned drab with dark mid-rib; Light Grizzle, brownish-grey, dark mid-rib, light tip; Pale Greyish-Blue, a lovely tint with dark mid-ribs; Light Badger, dark grey centre and mid-rib with a sulphur edge and point; Furnace, a very dark centre and mid-rib with light orange sides; Red-Breasted Red, a fine, clear, bright orange with a sheen of light carmine; Honeydew, a soft, light, stone-grey with a lighter edge of yellowish-buff; Dark Blue, a fine, rather blackish, indigo with a darker mid-rib; Ginger (for the Ginger Quill), a light, yellowish-cinnamon. Plum Red Duns, Red Grizzles, Blue Grizzles, Stone Grizzles, Honey Dun, Heather Dun, Grizzle-Bronze-Blue Dun (very rare) and, of course, the Honey Dun – a hackle with a dun centre with outer edges ranging from pale honey to a deep bronze colour. I could discourse on this theme for many hundreds of words, but can do no better than let Weir have the last word: 'Then comes the wonder, being so admired, as to why they are not more kept? Far surpassing in form and beauty as they long have, and still do, many of the breeds ordinarily cared for simply because they are pleasing to the eye. Then why not these elegancies clothed in tender half-toned loveliness – why not?'

Well, as we all know, modern life being what it is, indulgencies of this nature are almost impossible, but the greater tragedy is that with the vast amount of land and money devoted to the production of poultry today, there is practically nobody interested in producing these magnificent birds, even if only to keep breeds in existence.

The home breeder

However, this does not mean that among the angling fraternity there are not those who still have sufficient interest to continue the work carried on in the last century, and one of these is Timothy Benn, chairman of the publishing firm, Ernest Benn Ltd. The following are his notes on the breeding of Old English Game fowl, which could contribute to their not being included in the same category as the Dodo.

Perhaps the best answer to the shortage of good quality hackles for fly tying is to grow one's own.

There are numerous breeds of hen, but one – the Old English Game fowl – had advantages for the fly dresser. Old English Game are hard feathered, and most strains will produce good quality hackles. Furthermore, they 'throw' a wider range of colours than almost any other breed, ranging from reds to blacks, creams, and priceless blues with numerous mutations in between.

Most fly tyers who breed hens will probably want to concentrate on producing blue dun hackles, taking the reds and Greenwells and other colours which occur, as a bonus. (Even the Brown Leghorn will produce some of the finest Greenwells if used for breeding purposes.) If blues *are* the objective, a further point in favour of 'Old English' (what a marvellous but fast disappearing nomenclature) is that although they are difficult to find, they are not so rare as most of the other breeds which produce blue neck feathers. So start with these if possible. The biggest problem at the outset is to find good breeding stock. Try to locate someone who keeps Old English or other fancy breeds through your local paper or one of the farming magazines; a show with a poultry section; or by asking round among local farmers or gypsy encampments. Once contacts are made, the chances are that they will know someone who keeps O.E.G. even if they do not do so themselves. If a breeder will not part with stock, he may, perhaps, nevertheless be prepared to sell fertile eggs for hatching.

Get at least two or three hens and a cock for the first breeding pen and if blue is the objective, the birds should have as much blue in their feathers as possible. Indeed, the more blue there is in the pen, the shorter will be the time taken to produce a strain which regularly 'throws' a high proportion of this colour. Unfortunately, serious breeders very seldom keep blue cocks or hens as they are not popular on the show bench, but it is worth looking hard for blues before settling for and breeding any other colour. Look also for birds which stand up proudly, have bright beady eyes and, preferably, dark legs.

Any small hen house with a couple of nesting boxes and perch two feet off the ground will be adequate to start with. Game fowl do best if allowed completely free range in an orchard or field, but if this is not practicable, provide the biggest area possible for the birds to run in, with plenty of sunlight. In subsequent years smaller runs will be needed for the breeding pens. A word of warning here. Game fowl are the old cock-fighting breed. Whether or not cock-fighting still goes on, the ownership of fighting birds is still a status symbol amongst the gypsy-cum-scrap-dealing fraternity, so keep the pen out of sight of any road or casual caller. Otherwise there is the danger of waking up one morning, as I once did, to find all the birds gone! Similarly, take precautions against foxes, and as Game fowl fly very well, clip the primary feathers on one wing of each bird every ten months or so.

When a good strain is eventually established, put the odd bird out with other poultrymen in the area. If a fox – or worse – gets at the pen, the work is not all lost overnight.

Hatch under a broody hen rather than in an incubator as this method seems to give a better yield, and rearing on is subsequently easier. Do not wait for one of the breeding stock to go broody, but ask around amongst people who keep free-range hens until you find one with a broody. Start looking early – mid-March is not too soon – as it can take some weeks to find one. Make up breeding pens three months before setting the eggs, and never less than three weeks before so doing. Collect the eggs twice daily, see that they are clean, and mark the date on them with a pencil. Only well-shaped eggs with nice textured shells should be kept for setting, and they should be stored at an even temperature of 60°F.

When the broody has been found, drill some air holes in an old tea chest, put it in a quiet well-sheltered corner, and line it with straw. Have a piece of board ready to go over the front. Settle the broody for twenty-four hours on china eggs to make sure she will sit 'tight' and then put eleven to thirteen eggs under her, preferably just before it gets dark. The eggs should be not more then ten days old.

Let the broody off twice a day for food and water, ten minutes each morning and evening being about right. The eggs will hatch in twenty-one days. Thirty-six hours after the first chick has appeared, remove the straw and any unhatched eggs and substitute a layer of sawdust, wood shavings, or dry earth.

The chicks should have a small run of eight to ten feet long, and three feet wide in front of their coop, and this should be put in a warm, sheltered corner. They should not be fed during their first twenty-four hours, but after this will need feeding at two to four hour intervals with a good chick feed. This can be bought from any corn merchant. They need a good supply of fresh water, too. Put a half-brick in both the food and water dishes to prevent a chick turning one over and getting trapped underneath it. Keep the water in a shallow bowl, otherwise one unfortunate at least will drown itself. Move the coop regularly to fresh ground.

The chicks will grow rapidly, and after eight weeks can be started on layers mash and household scraps. Allow a plentiful supply of grit, too, and be sure to keep the feeding and water troughs clean. At ten to twelve weeks the chicks can be separated from the broody, and soon after will be ready to go out into the bigger pen. If they go into the breeding stock, watch carefully for cannibalism, and separate any birds which show such tendencies. It if does persist, take advice from a professional poultryman on debeaking.

Between six and seven months the main feathers come through, so by this time one knows not only how many cockerels have been produced, but also their colours. There are often surprises at this stage with birds which had previously promised to have exceptionally fine colouring turning out to be indifferent, and vice versa. If fed well on good quality layers mash and scraps, plus corn, some birds will have really fine hackles by twelve to fourteen months, sometimes as good or better than the hackles on a three-year-old bird which has been left to fend for itself free-range.

Between thirty and sixty hackles can be plucked from each of the birds which are kept and surprisingly they take little or no notice of this – after all they will lose them all at their next moult, anyway. Plucking can be carried out twice a year, in the winter months soon after the new hackles have come through, and/or in the summer when some will have taken on a brassy tinge from the sun. Keep both the neck and saddle from birds which are killed.

Cut the outer layer of skin under the chin down to, and round, the base of the neck and also round the crown of the head, ensuring that the small hackles are included. Then carefully peel off the cape. Stretch it tightly and pin on to a

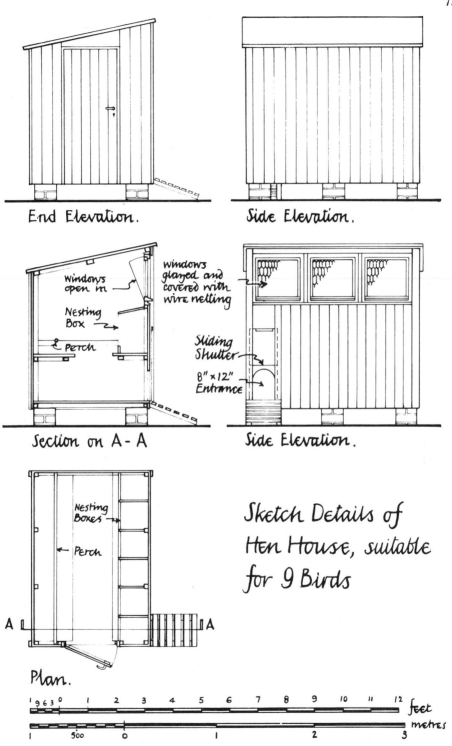

End Elevation.

Side Elevation.

windows
open in

Nesting
Box

Perch

windows
glazed and
covered with
wire netting

Sliding
Shutter

8" × 12"
Entrance

Section on A - A

Side Elevation.

Nesting
Boxes

Perch

A

A

Plan.

Sketch Details of
Hen House, suitable
for 9 Birds

1 9 6 3 0   1   2   3   4   5   6   7   8   9   10   11   12   feet

1   500   0   1   2   3   metres

piece of board, hackles down, and it will cure in about three weeks if left in a warm, dry place. Some breeders sprinkle borax or pyrethrum powder on the neck after it is pinned out, to help in the drying process. (More detailed instructions are given in Chapter 20.)

Breed only from the very best birds of one-year-old plus. Aim for colour first, then for quality and shape of hackle. Select birds with hackles which are long, and which show bright and glassy against the light. Hackle points should be short, straight and springy. Colour markings should be uniform, and not blurred. Avoid birds which have too much chalkiness on the reverse of the hackle, or which have too soft a web in the centre.

One of the fascinations of breeding Game fowl is that they do not invariably 'throw' true. There is always a good deal of anticipation in looking for the results which will come from the different crossings. In attempting to fix any particular colour strain, breed tightly among initial birds. On the infrequent occasions when a hen or cock is brought in from outside, make sure it comes from a consistent colour strain if the aim is to perpetuate that colour. If it comes from a mixed colour background, its offspring will probably be mixed.

If the objective is to produce blues, several earlier writers have suggested avoiding black in the breeding pen, as this colour may otherwise come through too strongly. One drawback to blues is that they tend to be softer in the hackle than some of the other colours, and to counter this the introduction of the occasional bird with red in its cape has been recommended.

Last, but not least, buy a good book on poultry keeping to help with the more fundamental and detailed aspects of looking after the birds; and one last comment – if it is more satisfying to catch a fish on a fly of one's own tying, how much more pleasure to tie the fly with a hackle of one's own breeding.

Cock hackles
(Supply, demand and substitutes)

Of course, it will not be possible for everyone who wants a special type of hackle to breed his own birds, consequently, ways and means have to be found to enable every fly tyer to get at least some of the special hackles he needs for favourite patterns.

To understand the problem fully, it is necessary to know the circumstances affecting supply, the reasons for shortages of some types, and the best methods of overcoming these shortages.

In the first place, some of the more popular types are freaks, which means that birds cannot be bred to guarantee a certain type of hackle. Within this range of types we have the furnace hackles required for the popular Greenwell's Glory, red/black for Coch-y-Bonddu, and badger for Grey Duster and other flies. All these have one common feature – a black centre – and the tips of the hackles are also sometimes black. They are the outcome of crossing various strains of birds, usually by the introduction of O.E.G. breeds into the flocks.

The main strains concentrated on by breeders for best egg- and flesh-producing results, are Red and Light Sussex, the Blacks and O.E.G. strains being introduced to improve the breed. The resulting birds, therefore, are nearly all Reds or Light Sussex, with now and again the improving breed cropping up in the plumage. A good furnace or a good badger may crop up only once in several thousand birds, which is the reason for the small number of these rare types, compared with the many hundreds of plain colours.

While breeders concentrate on these, to them, more profitable types, the number of freaks must continue to grow less. Added to this, is the fact that many of the old breeds are no longer encouraged, which is the reason that Plymouth Rock (grizzle) hackles are now as scarce as are the coveted blue duns, iron blues, honey duns, etc.

Although there must be many birds killed every year which would supply us with the hackles we require, modern methods of storing (cold store) and machinery plucking, render the hackles useless to the fly tyer. Many of them would be useless anyway, as few birds are allowed to reach the maturity that produces the hard hackles so necessary for the dry fly.

With the greatly increased production of table birds, it might be thought that there would be plenty of hackles for the fly tyer, but unfortunately this is not the case at all. The modern system of producing 'broilers' results in birds covered by nothing but a stubbly growth, absolutely useless for our purposes.

Before the war, the British poultry market supplied practically all the hackles we used, but the previously-mentioned circumstances have reduced this source of supply to a mere trickle. We also obtained many from what are now known as Iron Curtain countries, and even if these became available once again, no doubt we would find that they also have adopted the new methods of plucking and storing.

Consequently, new sources of supply had to be found, and the majority of our hackles now come from the East. Although quite a large number of the capes of hackles received from this source are excellent for dry flies, the range of types is very limited. We must count our blessings, however, because if it were not for this source of supply there would not be enough good hackles of any kind to go round, and those available would be almost priceless. We can but hope that modern methods will not reach that part of the world for some time. Even now, it is noticeable that the strains are getting more concentrated, and the number of 'freaks' growing smaller.

In an effort to overcome some of these shortages, dyed substitutes are taking the place of the blue dun and dun types, but it is of course, impossible to dye a badger, and in any case there are not enough badgers to spare for dyeing furnace.

The only ways to overcome the shortage of the freak hackles are (1) use larger hackles; (2) cut hackles; or (3) resort to a substitute. It is almost impossible to tell that the resulting fly has not been tied with a black-centred hackle, and although I know that the idea does not meet with the approval of purists, I can but ask, 'What else are we to do?'

My idea for a substitute sprang from the method I had seen used by several fly tyers, amateur and professional, which incorporated a small, short-fibred black hackle with a red, white or ginger hackle, the black hackle being used, of course, to simulate the black centre. I replaced the black hackle with a strand of black ostrich herl, and found it most effective. If one wishes to tie a Greenwell the method is as follows.

Form the body with rib – with a tail if required, leaving plenty of room at the eye end of the hook. Tie in the strand of ostrich herl close up to the body and continue winding the silk until the eye is nearly reached. Tie in the ginger hackle and wind the silk back to the ostrich herl. Wind the hackle up to the ostrich herl, tie in its tip and cut off the surplus. Wind the tying silk back through the hackle to the eye. Now wind the herl through the hackle to the eye, holding it as taut as possible so that the hackle fibres are not disturbed too much. When the eye is reached, tie in the herl and cut off the surplus. Finish off the fly with the usual whip finish.

The amount of black centre is, of course, governed by the number of turns given to the herl, and, for a lightly dressed fly, one turn at the back of the hackle, one or two through the hackle, and one in the front are all that is necessary.

Flies requiring a badger or a furnace hackle are tied in the same manner, using a white or a red hackle. Winged dry flies can also be tied, the wings being put on before the hackle and herl.

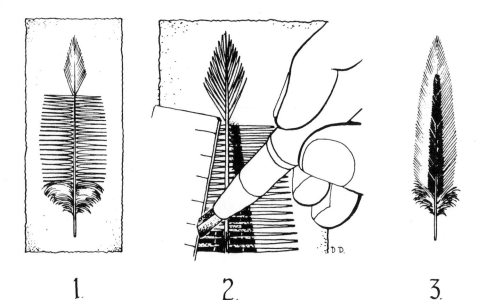

1.   2.   3.

Wet flies are treated in the same manner, by using hen hackles, or soft cock hackles.

Artificial colouring of hackles has also been tried, but this was always a difficult task with the black-centred hackles, although some fair results were achieved with barred ones. This was done by sealing off parts of the hackles so that the dye only affected the exposed parts, but results were far from natural-looking, and any dye seeping into the sealed off parts ruined the whole effect or just produced a mess.

The method I am going to describe here has none of these drawbacks, and produces the most natural-looking artificially-coloured hackles I have ever seen. Flies I have tied with them would defy any attempts to say that they were made other than with natural-marked hackles, the artificial colouring is waterproof and, as far as I have been able to ascertain to date, the spirit base of the colouring used seems to enhance the quality of the hackle. This appears to be due to the fact that the usually absorbent centre web of the hackle soaks up most of the spirit colouring, thus becoming waterproof itself. In addition, the colours are so fast that I have been unable to make them run even when washed in hot water a few minutes after they have been processed. It seems to me that we have made quite a breakthrough in the solving of the rarer hackle shortage. The process is illustrated below.

I have no wish to take the credit for the discovery: all I have done is to give it a thorough testing and ascertain its potential in various directions. I was started off along these lines by Geoffrey Bucknall, who very kindly passed the idea on to me to develop and publicise as I saw fit. He first thought of the artificial colouring of feathers, etc., when he discovered that a felt-tipped pen was ideal for dyeing stripped

4.   5.   6.

peacock quills used for quill-bodied flies. A quick run up and down the exposed side of the quill after stripping, and before tying in, of course, was all that was necessary, and it was this that made him suggest to me that it could be a useful idea for artificially marking hackles. I only had to evolve a method of procedure which would produce an even and natural-looking bar or stripe, whichever was required, and in the quickest possible time. I also had to decide which type of felt-tipped pen was best for the job.

There are several kinds of these pens on the market, and the one I found most useful was the stubby Magic Marker, which has a rather broad square tip, cut obliquely. This enables one to make either a fine or a heavy mark, which is very useful when making stripes which are broad at the base of the hackle and fine at the tip.

The fine, round-tipped, long felt pens are also quite useful, particularly when marking very small hackles, but they are not quite as generous in dispensing the waterproof ink.

Before starting to mark the hackles, there are two important points to remember. Hackles requiring a centre stripe should have the fibres drawn to right-angles to the stem, as in Fig. 1, and those which are to be used for cross-barring should be left in the natural position, as in Fig. 4.

To ensure good penetration of the colour, always work on an absorbent surface – blotting-paper for instance, or old newspaper.

To achieve a neat straight edge to the centre bar, use a straight-edge ruler (wood or metal), aligned to taper as Fig. 2.

The colouring is applied by a series of dots, and gaps are filled in by further dotting. Trying to draw a line along the hackle only drags the fibres, and the result is an uneven edge to the centre line. Fig. 3 gives some idea of how the hackle should look on completion.

If the centre stripe is not as dark as you would like, turn the hackle over and repeat the process on the back. This is one way we can improve on Nature, as all natural hackles are lighter on the back than on the front. In fact, this 'chalkiness' has always been a drawback on naturals.

If a black tip is required on the edges of the fibres (the true Coch-y-Bonddu marking), the straight-edge should cover the whole of the hackle except the extreme tips, and the tips should be dotted as well.

A cross-barred hackle, such as a grizzle, is produced in the same manner, using the undisturbed hackle as described above, but dotting horizontally, of course. These hackles should also be turned over if a darker effect is required, and slightly heavier dotting at the centre of each bar, where the fibres meet the stem, produces a very natural effect. In fact, flies tied with these hackles have been passed as 'naturals' by experienced members of our staff who have spent many years handling hackles of every colour and quality (Figs. 5 and 6).

I know there are many who will still prefer to use the natural-coloured hackles, and insist that it is not possible to improve on Nature. This may be partly true, but I think that the ideas I have described here are as near as we are likely to get artificially, and of course quantity is only limited by the number of plain-coloured hackles that need to be transformed. There is no shortage of reds, light or dark, for producing Greenwell's and Coch-y-Bonddus, and it is rarely that one is unable to obtain white hackles, either loose or in cape form, for grizzle or badger.

With regard to time, I have estimated that it takes about the same time to mark one side of a hackle as it does to strip the flue from a peacock herl when making quill-bodied flies. It varies, of course, according to the size of hackle being marked.

One final comment. The method does not have to be restricted to the special hackles I have mentioned, but could also be applied to hackles of every hue and used for many different purposes. In fact, a very good small streamer fly imitation of a perch fry was obtained by tying two dark ginger hackles alongside the shank, after they had been cross-barred as for a grizzle hackle. The result was most natural, and in this case was better than using the natural cree hackle one would normally think of for this purpose.

As this immediately starts one thinking about Badger Duns, Grizzle Duns, and the other possiblities of using artificial colouring, the enormous scope of this new method will be more readily grasped.

Try it for yourself and see!

The only snag we have come up against so far, is that although the marking ink is waterproof, floatants of the Mucilin type can cause the colour to run. To overcome this, I first treat my hackles with the floatant, allow them to dry, and then carry out the marking. When the flies are finished, I apply more floatant using an aerosol type of applicator, and by this means have been able to retain all the colour with only imperceptible effect from the floatant. The better quality hackles one uses, the less floatant one needs of course.

The hackle cape

The cape is the best form in which to purchase hackles, the reasons being (1) convenience of storage, (2) accessibility for size selection, and, last but not least, (3) convenience for quality assessment.

As far as (1) is concerned, whole capes can be stored in separate bags, either PVC or cellophane, each bag containing some recommended parasite repellent.

The illustration on page 80 explains (2), although it must be borne in mind that not every cape is alike. This means that the lines A–H are approximations, and on a first-class quality cape, for example, the line A would be higher up, the rest of the lines moving up in proportion. In other words, there would be a higher proportion of good-quality, small hackles for dry fly purposes.

Quality assessment is only acquired by experience, but this does not take long. To ascertain quality, the cape should be folded backwards so that some of the hackles stand out, and they are then held to the light to see how much centre-web is present. The less centre-web, the more suited are the hackles for dry fly work. Whilst the cape is still folded, individual hackles should be bent and then released. Good dry-fly hackles will spring back like a watch spring, while softer wet-fly ones have a more 'sloppy' reaction. A good comparison is to place a hen's hackle alongside a good-quality cock's hackle. This will give the two extremes, the hen's hackle being wide, heavily 'webbed', and with a slow reaction when given the 'watch-spring' test. Hen's hackles are invariably used for wet flies, but poor-quality cock hackles can be also, especially if used on large flies which will be fished in fast water. The fact that most salmon flies use hackles of this nature is an illustration of what I mean.

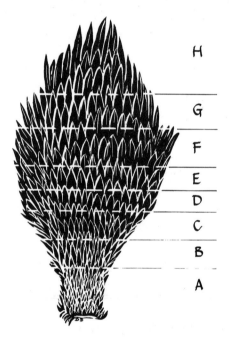

H

G

F

E

D

C

B

A

The very best type of 'dry-fly quality' cape would be from an oldish bird killed at the right time (i.e. when the bird is in full plumage) and would be web-free right up into the largest hackles. It is the hackles from this type of cape which can be used for large 'dapping' flies, and the dry salmon flies which are quite popular in North America.

Another good feature of the cape is the quality and type of the side hackles. These are the ones which run up the side of each cape at its widest point, and they have a very similar quality to spade hackles, in that they are very short, have very long, stiff fibres, and are ideally suited to making sturdy tail whisks for dry flies. They can also be used for hackle-point wings, particularly for mayflies, and by using just a couple of turns of the long, spiky hackle fibres they make ideal hackles for spiders.

One final advantage the cape has over loose hackles, is the availability it gives of hackles in pairs. This means that two hackles of exactly the same type, colour and size can be selected for use on streamer flies and, of course, for hackle-point wings; and as far as the streamer wings are concerned, nearly all the hackles on any cape can be used, provided they are the right length.

As I said earlier, the hackles contained within the lineal markings on the drawing are approximations, but generally speaking the following gradations apply.

A Very small hackles for the smallest flies – size 18 and smaller – and very small hackle-point wings.

B Same as A, but including sizes up to 14. Body hackles for sedge patterns also come within this range.

C Hackles for sizes 12–16 hooks, larger spent wings, hackle-point wings, and hackles for the smaller spiders.

D Hackles for sizes 10–14 hooks, and the same applications as C. It is in this range that we would start selecting hackles for the smaller streamer flies, and also for body hackles for mayflies and small salmon flies.

E Hackles for sizes 8–12 hooks, spent wings or mayflies, body hackles for salmon flies and also hackles for small salmon flies. Hackles for largish lake flies would come from this range, and also for sea-trout flies.

F Hackles for sizes 4–6 hooks, mostly salmon, sea- and lake-trout flies, and for use as hackle fibre wings, particularly on spent mayflies. It is also from these size ranges that we would obtain our hackles for 'dapping' flies and dry salmon flies.

G Hackles for sizes 4–1/0 hooks, salmon flies, of course, and large 'collar' type hackles for hair-winged and streamer flies. This is also a good area for streamer wings.

H Hackles for very large salmon flies.

As it often happens that one is not able to obtain hackles on the cape, some guide relating hackle length to hook size is necessary. The list of sizes on page 82 is given with reservations, as the length of hackle required depends entirely upon the length of the fibres on the hackle. Invariably, a hackle from an old bird will have much shorter fibres in comparison with its length than will that of a hackle from a young bird.

HACKLE SIZE CHART
(Hen hackles should be about $\frac{1}{2}$ in. smaller)

Hook sizes		Cock hackles	
New Nos.	*Old Nos.*	HACKLE FLIES – (TROUT) – WINGED FLIES	
000	17		
00	16	1 in.–$1\frac{1}{4}$ in.	$\frac{1}{2}$ in.–1 in.
0	15		
1	14		
2	13	$1\frac{1}{4}$ in.–$1\frac{1}{2}$ in.	1 in.–$1\frac{1}{4}$ in.
3	12		
4	11	SEA-TROUT FLIES	LAKE-TROUT FLIES
5	10	$1\frac{1}{2}$ in.–$1\frac{3}{4}$ in.	$1\frac{1}{4}$ in.–$1\frac{1}{2}$ in.
6	9		
7	8		
8	7	$1\frac{3}{4}$ in.–$2\frac{1}{4}$ in.	$1\frac{1}{2}$ in.–2 in.
9	6		

The tyer of wet flies is much more easily supplied, as he does not require the stiff cock's hackles. The softer hen's hackles, which are much more plentiful than their male counterpart, make for easier entry of the fly into the water, although a not-too-stiff cock's hackle should be used if more 'life' is required, especially in fast water.

We have produced a colour plate showing the hackles in general use (see plate 8) whilst the shades of blue dun, dun, olive, etc., will be found in the chart of dye shades (plate 14). I am also adding the list on page 83, with a description of the hackle concerned, to enable the reader to recognise any that come his way.

There are also many patterns of flies that call for feathers for use as 'hackles' from birds other than poultry, and it is rarely that any difficulty is experienced in obtaining these. The following list should cover the requirements of the most exacting collector.

Starling body feathers For the hackle of Black Gnat and midges.

Partridge brown back feather A very useful feather, providing the hackle of the March Brown, Partridge and Orange, whisks for tails, hackles of nymphs and spiders, and also for several patterns of mayflies. (Illustrated in plate 9.)

Partridge grey breast feather A very similar feather to the above, used for the hackle of the Partridge and Yellow and for the hackles of mayflies. It is used dyed and undyed for the latter, yellow being the most popular colour.

French partridge breast feather This is a smoky-blue feather, barred at its tip. It is only used for mayflies, dyed and undyed. It is very popular in Ireland, usually

Grizzle	Alternate bars of black and white. From the Plymouth Rock breed.
Cree	Alternating bars of black and red, sometimes with flecks of white. The result of crossing Plymouth Rock with Rhode Island Red poultry. A lighter variation is referred to as Ginger Chinchilla or Honey/Grizzle.
Reds (Brown)	From the Rhode Island Red breed.
Red Game	Old English Game breed – see 'History of the Hackle', page 67.
Badger	A black-centred hackle, sometimes with black outer tips also.
Furnace	Black centre with red outer fibres.
Coch-y-Bonddu	As Furnace, but with edges of the outer fibres tipped with black.
Greenwell	Black centre with ginger outer fibres. Named after the fly Greenwell's Glory.
Honey	A pale gingery-buff, but the shades can range from natural unrefined honey (from the bees), to the warm bronze of the refined variety.
Blue Dun	Slate grey.
Iron Blue	Very dark slate grey, or 'inky'.
Dun	Mouse-coloured.
Honey Dun & Honey Blue Dun	Dun or blue dun-centred feathers, with honey tips as described above.
Rusty Dun & Rusty Blue Dun	Dun or blue dun-centred feathers with the deepest honey tips described above.

I hope that white, black, buff and ginger will require no description from me, especially as the last two are illustrated.

---

dyed green, where a large bushy fly is tied, with plenty of body and hackle. (Illustrated in plate 9.)

Snipe rump feathers Used as hackles for the Snipe series of flies, the best known being the Snipe and Purple.

Cock pheasant neck feather Used for the hackle of the Bracken Clock. (Illustrated in plate 9.)

Hen pheasant neck feather There are one or two patterns of wet mayflies that use this feather, but it has few other uses. (Illustrated in plate 9.)

Hen pheasant flank feather This is used rarely in Great Britain, but often in New Zealand, as a substitute for bittern. It forms the hackle of the Matuka, which is probably one of the best-known flies in that part of the world. (Illustrated in plate 9.)

Grouse poult feathers These are under-coverts from the wing, and can be obtained only from very young grouse. They form the hackle of the Poult Bloa.

Grey mallard duck breast and flank feathers (grey drake). These are obtainable in a large range of sizes varying in length from about 1 in. to 4 in. The smallest sizes are used for fan-wings on mayflies, and the larger for the hackles of wet mayflies. They are obtainable dyed and undyed, and the natural coloration lends itself to the imitation of the Green Drake. They are also dyed to provide substitutes for the rare summer duck, Egyptian goose and mandarin duck feathers. (Illustrated in plate 10.)

Egyptian goose breast feathers These are lightly barred feathers, varying in colour from pale buff to brown. They are used for the wings and hackles of some patterns of mayflies.

Summer duck (Carolina wood-duck) flank feathers These are also lightly barred brown feathers, but of a richer colour than the Egyptian goose. They are also used as hackles for mayflies, and for many American patterns.

Mandarin duck flank feathers Almost an exact duplicate of summer duck flank feathers, and extensively used as a substitute for them. Although not in plentiful supply, they are easier to get than summer duck.

Woodcock body feathers, and lesser coverts from wings Used as hackles for mayflies and nymphs, etc., and for the hackled patterns of the Woodcock series of flies – Woodcock and Yellow, etc.

Grouse body feathers, and lesser coverts from wings Also used for mayflies and nymphs, etc., and for the hackled patterns of the Grouse series of lake- and sea-trout flies – Grouse and Claret, etc. (Illustrated in plate 9.)

Jay wing blue lesser coverts These are used as hackles for many well-known patterns of lake-, sea-trout and salmon flies such as the Invicta, Connemara Black, Thunder and Lightning, etc. Being stiff feathers, they are rather difficult to use as hackles. The quill part has to be stripped as thinly as possible to enable them to be tied and wound properly, or bunches of fibres are applied as 'false' hackles.

Jackdaw grey neck feathers These range from a smoky grey to almost black, and are used for wet fly versions of the Iron Blue, and also the Dark Watchet.

Hackles can also be obtained from the wings of other birds, and it is the under-coverts and marginal coverts that are used. Coot, waterhen, starling, cock and hen pheasant, partridge and lapwing are but a few that can be used.

11

Materials for salmon flies

Many of the materials used for salmon flies come from the range of those used for trout flies, especially as far as tinsels, silks, body materials and hackles are concerned.

However, as many salmon fly requirements are of a completely specialised nature, I have thought it better to keep them separate.

Hackles

As far as body hackles are concerned, it is usually the common poultry hackle that is utilised, mostly in dyed colours, but sometimes using badger, grizzle or furnace. There is little difficulty in obtaining hackles for salmon flies, owing to the fact that there are always plenty of the larger sizes left after the smaller ones have been extracted for trout fly tying.

Other feathers used for body hackles are heron (grey and black) for Spey and Dee strip-wing flies, and the fluffy feathers from the thigh of the golden eagle, which are also used for some patterns of Dee strip-wing flies. The golden eagle hackles are very difficult to obtain, but a very good substitute is found in turkey marabou plumes dyed the required shades.

The scale given below will give the tyer some idea of the size of poultry hackles to be used on the different sizes of hooks. They are only approximate sizes of course, as the size of the hackle to be used is regulated not by its length, but by the length of the fibres on it.

Hook numbers	Hackle sizes (in.)	Hook numbers	Hackle sizes (in.)
5	2	2/0	$3\frac{3}{4}$
4	$2\frac{1}{4}$	3/0	4
3	$2\frac{1}{2}$	4/0	$4\frac{1}{4}$
2	$2\frac{3}{4}$	5/0	$4\frac{1}{2}$
1	3	6/0	5
$1\frac{1}{2}$	$3\frac{1}{4}$	7/0	$5\frac{1}{2}$
1/0	$3\frac{1}{2}$	8/0	6

The feathers used for throat hackles are usually much coarser fibred than those used for body hackles, although one or two patterns call for poultry hackles. The Durham Ranger is one of these, and requires a light blue cock's hackle for the throat. The coarse fibred hackles most in general use are:

Guinea fowl (gallena) spotted throat, breast and flank feathers.
Partridge brown back and grey breast feathers.
Grouse breast and rump.
Woodcock back and rump.
Teal breast feathers.
Widgeon neck feathers.
Golden pheasant red breast and yellow back feathers.
Jay, blue lesser wing coverts.

Wings

This is the most varied section of the salmon fly tyers' materials, owing to the fact that some flies of the 'mixed' or 'built' wing type often require strips from half a dozen or more different feathers. The strips are very narrow, of course, varying in thickness from one to three fibres according to the size of fly being tied. This means, therefore, that strips for quite a large number of flies can be taken from each feather, and this does much to offset the original outlay on this part of one's collection.

Golden pheasant tippet neck feathers (Illustrated in plate 10). These are orange with two black bars, and form the base of several salmon fly wings. They cannot be 'married' with fibres from other feathers, so tippet fibres are tied in before the rest of the wing. Whole feathers of tippet are used back to back for the wings of such patterns as the Durham Ranger and Orange Parson.

Golden pheasant crest feathers (Illustrated in plate 10.) Although the main functions of these feathers is to form the tails and toppings of many patterns, there are one or two flies that have wings composed entirely of them. They are a bright translucent golden yellow. Regardless of the use to which they are put, golden pheasant crest feathers are usually referred to as 'toppings', especially in the dressings.

Golden pheasant tail feathers These are black/brown mottled centre tail feathers, and their fibres 'marry' well with fibres from other feathers. They have to be purchased in pairs as there is no true centre tail on the golden pheasant. This means that the fibres on one side of each tail feather are shorter than those on the other side of the quill.

Goose shoulder feathers These can be obtained either white or dyed, the most usual colours being red, blue, yellow, green and orange. They are used in all mixed- or built-wing patterns. Used as a substitute for swan.

Amherst pheasant tail feathers There are not many British patterns that call for these feathers, but they are popular in Canada, Iceland and Norway. They are similar in shape to golden pheasant tails, but are larger and have black and silver markings instead of black and brown.

Speckled bustard wing quills These feathers are required for many patterns but, unfortunately, supplies are very limited. The grey speckled and oak brown speckled feathers from the wing of the turkey make excellent substitutes.

Florican bustard wing quill This is a 'tiger-striped' quill, the stripes being of black and buff.

Guinea fowl wing and tail feathers These are dark grey feathers with white spots. They are used in one or two patterns, but, owing to the shortness of their fibres, they cannot be used on very large hooks.

Hen pheasant tail feathers (Illustrated in plate 5.) These are not used very often, one of the few patterns being the March Brown. They are true centre tails, which means that pairs of wings can be made from single feathers.

Turkey wing and tail feathers The turkey supplies us with many feathers for salmon flies, the most useful being the tails, of which there are a large variety:

Dark with white tip, for Jock Scott and Dusty Miller, etc.
Grey mottled, for Silver Doctor and Yellow Eagle, etc.
Plain cinnamon brown, for Akroyd, etc.
Brown mottled, for Blue Charm, etc.
White and dyed. These are used as a substitute for swan, especially on very large patterns.

Grey mallard drake (wild duck) flank feathers These are light grey feathers with slightly darker grey bars. They are sometimes used as a substitute for pintail flank feathers (illustrated in plate 10).

Brown mallard drake shoulder feathers (Illustrated in plate 10.) These are brown speckled feathers, the fibres varying in colour from deep brown at the tips to grey at the roots. They are used on nearly all standard patterns, forming the roof of the wing before the topping is put on. Some patterns have wings that consist solely of two strips of these feathers, a well-known one being the Thunder and Lightning.

Barred mandarin duck and barred summer duck flank feathers These are buff speckled feathers with heavy black and white bars at their tips. They are incorporated in the wings of many patterns, and sometimes used as sides. Now extremely scarce.

Peacock wing quills There are several patterns that call for these feathers, but, owing to their scarcity, buff mottled turkey tails are used as a substitute.

Pintail flank feathers These feathers have heavy black stripes on a pale grey background, and are similar to teal flank.

Teal duck flank feathers (Illustrated in plate 10.) These have heavy black bars on a white background. They are also used as hackles, the Akroyd being one pattern that makes use of them for this purpose.

Widgeon shoulder feathers Similar to the teal feathers but more finely marked. They are not quite as long in the fibre so are more suitable for small patterns, especially of the low-water type such as the Silver Blue.

Peacock 'sword' tail feathers (Illustrated in plate 5.) The herls from these tails are used in some wings, the Jock Scott requiring two or three. The Alexandra has wings that consist entirely of these herls.

Peacock 'eye' tail feathers (Illustrated in plate 5.) The herls from the 'eye' part of these tails are used, the Beauly Snow Fly being the most well-known pattern that requires them. The herls from the lower part of the feather are often used for bodies.

SIDES   Some of the feathers used for wings are also required as sides in some patterns. These are the pintail, teal, widgeon and barred mandarin duck or summer duck. Not many others are needed, and the following list (or their substitutes) should cover all general requirements:

> Blue chatterer (or blue kingfisher as a substitute).
> Indian (red) crow feathers.
> Toucan breast feathers.
> Jungle cock feathers.

CHEEKS   Smaller sizes of the above feathers are used as cheeks, the most useful being the blue chatterer and the Indian crow, or their substitutes.

TOPPING   With very few exceptions, this is a golden pheasant crest feather. Two of the exceptions are Amherst pheasant crests and peacock 'sword' herls. The function of the topping is not only to add to the attractiveness of the fly, but also to keep the wing in good shape.

HORNS   There is a modern tendency to omit these from the dressings, but if they are included they are obtained from the tail feathers of the macaw. These feathers are usually blue on the outer face and either red or yellow underneath. They are difficult to obtain, which is the main reason for their not being much used.

HEAD   The heads of nearly all salmon flies are finished off with black varnish, red being about the only other colour sometimes used. Some patterns call for wool or peacock herl heads, but their number is very small.

12

Tubes

The tube fly, as its name indicates, consists of a length of polythene or metal tubing, round which hair fibres from the tails of different animals are whipped. Orthodox salmon fly bodies are sometimes added to the tubes, and long-fibred hackles may be used in conjunction with the hair fibres, or even in place of them. Heron and guinea fowl hackles are good examples of feathers which may be used for this purpose.

The tube flies are fished in conjunction with a treble hook which is attached to the end of the leader. The tube is pushed down the leader tail first until it is stopped by the eye of the hook. For colour variations or increase in size, two tubes can be used instead of one, and Figs. 1 and 2 illustrate the two methods.

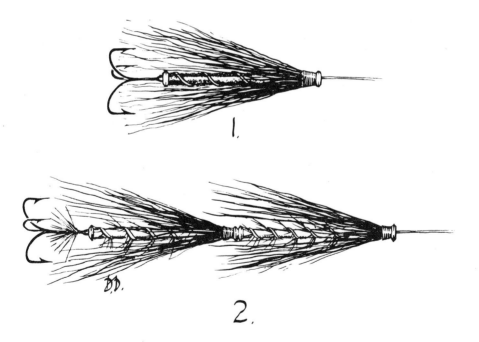

Ordinary fly-tying implements (including a vice) are all that are required to make tube flies, plus two or three sizes of tapered (no-eye) salmon hooks onto which the tubes can be pushed to facilitate the tying. I would suggest sizes 4, 2, 1, 1/0 and 3/0, as these should cope with most of the sizes of tubes one is likely to use. If a tube with a very large interior diameter is used, I suppose a special mount would have to be made for it if the flies are to be tied in a vice.

Types of slipstream tubes

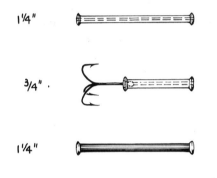

1¼"   A. Plastic tube with moulded ends which prevent the dressing from slipping off.

¾"   B. A stouter plastic tube with cavity in tail to take eye of treble hook so that it is always in perfect alignment.

1¼"   C. Plastic-lined aluminium tube which cannot chafe cast of 'skid' on surface of water.

There is also a fourth type, which is similar to type C but made of plastic-lined brass instead of aluminium to ensure rapid sinking. Sizes: $\frac{1}{2}$, $\frac{3}{4}$, 1, 1$\frac{1}{4}$, 1$\frac{1}{2}$, 2 in. (Suggested eyed treble hook sizes: Nos. 16, 15, 14, 13, 12 and 10.)

Dyes for dyed goods

KINGFISHER BLUE

LIGHT BLUE

DARK BLUE

BLUE (BLUE AND TEAL)

BRIGHT GREEN

GINGER

CINNAMON

SIENNA

FIERY BROWN

RED

BRIGHT YELLOW

YELLOW

NAPLES YELLOW

GOLDEN OLIVE

GREEN OLIVE

GREEN DRAKE

SUMMER DUCK

IRON BLUE

GREY

MOLE

Dyes for dyed goods

 INSECT GREEN

 DARK GREEN

 GREEN HIGHLANDER

 HOT ORANGE

 SCARLET

 CRIMSON

LIGHT CLARET

 DARK CLARET

 MAGENTA

LEMON YELLOW

 MEDIUM OLIVE

BROWN OLIVE

DARK OLIVE

 OLIVE DUN

PURPLE

DUN

 BLUE DUN

 SHERRY SPINNER

BEIGE

 GRANNOM GREEN

Dyes for dyed goods

13
Dyeing

The principles of dyeing materials for fly tying were first laid down in exact form by F. M. Halford in his book *Floating Flies and How to Dress Them*. Although he mentioned some of the older recipes, which used such ingredients as ebony chips, onion skin, black tea, copperas, logwood chips and potash, it was he who first approached a commercial house with a view to having a series of dyes produced that would give the fly tyer a required colour in a single operation. His ideas were accepted, and the basic colours originated by Halford are still obtainable in the shades stipulated by him. In the book, he gave nine basic colours each with four different shades, but in his *Modern Development of the Dry Fly*, this was extended to eighteen colours and a total of seventy-two shades.

The company responsible for producing the dyes was Messrs. E. Crawshaw & Co., and when they went out of business, Veniard's – then consisting of my late father and elder brother – reproduced the colours laid down by Halford. Subsequently other colours were added, forty-four in all, and by judicious mixing, one can realise a great number of permutations, all stemming from Halford's original conception of what was needed by the fly dresser.

Even his dyeing instructions have stood the test of time, showing change only in respect of the modern materials now available for washing the feathers and fixing the dye.

Dyeing one's own materials can be a most interesting part of our fly dressing procedure, bearing in mind the scope for experiment and the pleasure one can derive from achieving a particular result. Furthermore, it is not the messy business one might assume.

I have already mentioned how the old-fashioned (though effective) methods were transformed by the advent of specifically prepared dyes, and I will now explain the simplification this has produced.

Dyes can now be bought from any fishing tackle shop that stocks fly-tying materials, or from the firms specialising in the sale of these items.

As I said earlier, the two-score-plus number of colours is sufficient for all our needs, and as these dyes have not been adulterated like most textile dyes, they are very economical in use.

The only utensils necessary for the small quantities needed by the home fly dresser are a small aluminium milk saucepan and another slightly larger one. The smaller saucepan is perforated with little holes over the sides and bottom with an awl, transforming it into a colander. Or, if you wish, a wire potato-chip basket is ideal. This is to hold the material being dyed, and it will stand inside the larger utensil. This 'colander' will take quite a quantity of small feathers and any fur which is to be dyed, whilst larger feathers may be cut to fit into it. For dyeing large items such as hackle capes or animal tails, a larger pan will be needed, preferably of stainless steel. If you intend to do a lot of dyeing, two sets of utensils are advisable – one for dark colours and the other for light. Additional utensils are: a pan or bowl for soaking the material prior to dyeing, a pair of tongs for picking up material (those used by chefs can be used) and a stainless steel spoon.

The object of the colander is the easy control of the dyeing process, and inspection of material whilst the dyeing is going on. It also helps cleanliness, as the hands have no need to come in contact with the dye solution.

Furs and feathers have to be treated before dyeing, and the customary process is quite simple. Make a solution of soapsuds in the larger saucepan by dissolving good-quality soapflakes in hot water. If soapflakes are not available, we can nowadays make use of detergents and de-greasers which are thoroughly recommended, being quick to use, and very effective.

Place your feathers in the colander and immerse them in the soapy water for a few minutes. The feathers of wildfowl which have an in-built water repellent should be soaked much longer – say at least half to one hour. The feathers must now be well rinsed, and this is quite simple with the colander. Just lift it out of the pan of suds and place it in another containing clean, warm water, and repeat this until all traces of soap have been removed. Holding it under a running hot tap is even simpler.

The directions when using a detergent are as follows: draw enough hot water into a bowl to immerse the materials in. Add the detergent (we market Venpol for this purpose) and swish the water into a lather before adding the materials to be cleaned or dyed. Half a fluid ounce of Venpol to four pints of water (or 1 part in 60) is ideal. Allow soaking time according to the material (as mentioned previously).

Venpol is so pure that unless your material is very dirty, rinsing is not necessary prior to dyeing. It is not a de-greasing agent, but a very effective detergent, so use it sparingly.

If the material is only being cleaned, then it should be thoroughly rinsed in clean, warm water before being spread out to dry.

The use of a de-greaser is advised for removing the obstinate oil and grease from hair and feathers before dyeing, and is particularly recommended for bucktails, squirrel tails, goat hair, seal's fur, and all raw materials on the skin. It is difficult for dye to penetrate if any grease or natural oils are left on feathers or hairs, and a de-greaser ensures quick and uniform penetration of the dye, removes grease far better than any bleaching agent, ammonia, detergent or soapy water can alone, and will ensure fast, bright colours.

The directions for using de-greaser are as follows: prepare the bath of warm water as previously described (using Venpol), then add a 2% solution of de-greaser, or 1 part in 50. Soak the material in this solution and work the suds thoroughly. Leave to soak for at least an hour, then rinse in warm water.

If one is dyeing more obstinate types, such as greasy bucktails, proceed as follows to obtain a fast colour: soak them in the prepared solution as described *but do not rinse*. Remove the material and add the dye to this original solution. Replace the material and dye in the normal way adding the fixative when the desired shade is obtained, and rinsing afterwards in cold running water. Hackles on the skin should be processed by soaking in a solution of 2% de-greaser and water *only*. Rinse in warm water to remove the surface film before dyeing.

The foregoing instructions should meet all requirements as far as preparation of materials is concerned, and we now come to the actual dyeing process, which is the same for all materials, whatever way they have been prepared.

Half fill the larger saucepan with water, and stand it over a gentle heat. Add one quarter of a teaspoonful of dye powder to one quart of water for feathers from land birds, and double the quantity (half a teaspoonful) for feathers from waterfowl. Allow the solution to come to boiling point. Cold water should then be added to reduce the temperature, *as feathers must not be boiled.* Now immerse the colander containing the materials in the dye solution.

Leave the material in the solution for some minutes, then lift out the colander and add approximately one tablespoonful of setting agent to the solution. This should be acetic acid or vinegar. This will fix the colour quickly and care must now be taken to get the right shade. The colander is most useful here, as to inspect the material, all one has to do is lift it out of the larger saucepan. The water runs out through the holes leaving the material at the bottom for inspection. It must be remembered that the material will be lighter in colour when dry, and it may be necessary to add more dye to get a deeper shade. This again is quite simple with the colander, as it can be lifted out while more dye is added to the solution without its coming into contact with the material being dyed. You can get a very good idea of what shade the feathers have reached by inspecting the quills, or holding a single feather up to the light.

Having obtained the desired shade, remove the colander from the dye solution, and hold it under a cold water tap until all surplus dye is rinsed off. Press the material between cloth or newspaper to absorb most of the moisture, and then allow it to dry naturally, or over a gentle heat.

Shades of red, yellow, blue, etc., are quite straightforward, but a little experience is required to obtain the delicate shades of olives and duns. The tendency is to use too much dye and it is much better to start with a little and add more as necessary.

At this point, I would like to give special attention to the additional requirements of dyeing materials black. It is not as difficult as one might imagine, but a little more application is required. Firstly, at least double the amount of black dye should be used compared with that for colours, and the material should be left in the heated solution much longer. A good idea is to leave the dye-bath standing overnight to cool and by morning a rich glossy black should be obtained. Furthermore, it would be a waste of time to use white materials to dye black, as these can be used for the bright or softer colours. For instance, capes of red cock hackles, the darker the better, give a head start when dyeing black.

Having dyed our materials, we now have to bring them back to the natural sheen they had whilst still on the live animal or bird, and this is much simpler than one would imagine. Large commercial firms which have to dye quantities of feathers have a simple procedure which we are able to copy, even with the much smaller quantities with which we are concerned. It is as follows: the feathers that have been washed or dyed are placed in a revolving drum with holes in it, similar to our colander, underneath which hot air circulates, usually created by gas jets. The combination of hot air with movement dries the feathers, returns them to their natural shape and lustre, and leaves them immediately ready for use.

We can achieve the same results by replacing the revolving drum with a cardboard tray – the base of a shoe box or something similar will do. This is then held over a gas ring or burner and gently shaken to and fro, ensuring of course that the bottom of the box is not held so near the heat that it scorches. It is remarkable how quickly loose feathers regain their natural sheen by this simple operation.

In the same way, material on the skin such as hackle necks and bucktails, should be lightly beaten against the palm of one hand while being held above the gas ring or burner.

Of course the range of shades of any colour is infinite, and doing one's own dyeing enables one to test ideas.

As I said earlier, red hackles should be used to get black, and they will also dye claret, purple or fiery brown. Furthermore, it is not necessary to use absolutely pure white necks for the duns and olives. Those capes which have some darker markings, such as poor-coloured badger or grizzle, can be used, and this not only produces the broken colour that many of us prefer in our hackles, but is also a means of turning more or less useless hackles into something quite valuable. Using the blue and other dun dyes on cream or variant capes, such as the light ginger chinchilla, will produce honey duns and rusty duns, as will those capes we get now and again which have a white centre and a rusty edge.

To sum up, I will run over one or two of the more important factors in the simplest possible way:

1 Remove all traces of soap from feathers before putting them into the dye bath.
2 Never allow the material being dyed to boil, as this takes all the life out of it, particularly with hackles.
3 Always remove the material before adding more dye, otherwise there is a danger of 'spotting'.
4 Do not use a stronger dye bath than necessary. Extra dye can always be added if the shade is too light.
5 Rinse well after dyeing.
6 Never dry before a fierce heat, as this also will take the life out of the material.

Fluorescent dyes

These, of course, are comparatively new additions to our range of dyes, but the dyeing instructions are the same, with the exception that one does not have to use quite so much dye. The following notes will prove useful:

Hackles dye well and fluoresce excellently, and a large range of olives and duns is available by mixing the dyes. Do not attempt dark shades such as claret or sooty olive, for although you can dye your materials these and other dark colours, your fluorescence lessens in proportion to the depth of colour produced. I explain this in more detail in the next chapter. The same directions apply to furs, silks and wools, although some materials fluoresce better than others. Man-made fibres react very well, and mohair (Tibetan goat hair) produces bright shades also. Natural hair fibres such as seal's fur, bucktail and goat hair, do not fluoresce so brightly, so your dyed shades should be kept as light as possible.

Because of the colour range limitations, the number of fluorescent dyes is quite small, and consists of eight pastel shades. These are: white, yellow, orange, scarlet, blue, lime, pink and grey. But they can be mixed as an artist mixes his paints. For example, pink and orange will give salmon pink, lime and blue will give the green for Teal and Green, pink and blue will give magenta for Silver Wilkinson, and we have the grey, blue, green and yellow to mix for the duns and olives.

Under the fluoroscope, white will appear as blue, although the white material will not change colour when it is dyed. Grey will also fluoresce blue, and here the colour should be kept as light as possible to get the best fluorescent result. Pink, lime and blue should be kept as light as possible, but a really rich orange, scarlet and yellow can be obtained without masking the fluorescence in any way.

14

Fluorescent materials in fly tying

There must be few anglers who are not aware of a medium of attraction, not only in their sport, but also in everyday life. Examples may be seen on hoardings, buses, commercial vehicles and in shops. It takes the form, usually, of printed matter that stands out clearly in any surroundings, because of its brilliance.

The use of daylight fluorescent material for fly tying was first thought of by Eugene Burns, of America, during the Second World War, and now both the U.S.A. and Great Britain are producing these materials for use by the fly tyer.

Daylight fluorescent material, which we will call D.F.M., consists of specially treated fibres, and usually takes one of the three following forms: a thin floss, a wool yarn, or a chenille which is best described to the fly tyer as a 'herl' of silk.

It is also possible to obtain hackles and furs dyed with this medium, or the dyes to carry out one's own ideas.

First, a little simple theory. It has been suspected, and there is much to indicate it, that fish have sight which is sensitive to the light rays at the blue end of the spectrum. In fact, they may be able to record with their eyes, ultra-violet rays, or at any rate a different range of colours activated by ultra-violet rays. In order that humans may see the appearance of objects when exposed to these rays, special scientific instruments are needed, but the fish may see these effects with their normal sight. It is an interesting theory and a likely one. With D.F.M. we have a material which relies upon ultra-violet and blue and green light for its brilliance, and if it can be blended into the body of an imitation fly it may well be that an exact imitation, from a fishy point of view, might be possible. This would obviously benefit the trout fisherman.

In deep or coloured water, particularly moving water, no matter what degree of sight fish have, they must obviously be very limited in their seeing distance. All food they capture must therefore be such as they happen to see passing close to them, and such as they detect by other senses. As we are dealing with non-tasting or smelling foods, anglers must give the fish the best possible chance of seeing the offer. Fluorescent objects, capturing the very weakest of light rays no matter what their wave length, will automatically give the best chance. D.F.M. therefore is ideal for any lure to be used 'wet', and has potentialities for the sea-trout, salmon and wet fly trout angler.

Although much information has been gathered about the efficacy of D.F.M., one or two misconceptions have arisen. If I can dispel these, it may save many anglers from using flies which are supposed to be fluorescent, but which are not. For instance, I have read that on certain days fish would only take flies incorporating D.F.M. in the body or wings, and colours such as 'dark olive' and 'claret' were mentioned. I have even heard 'black' quoted in connection with fluorescent material. From experiments carried out during the production of the British materials, I know that it is only pastel shades of the primary colours that can be given to the materials. The colours found to react the best were: white, blue, yellow, lime green, orange, scarlet, pink and grey. Darker colours went black under the fluoroscope. The adding of a dark colour to a fluorescent material is the equivalent of giving a coat of paint to a piece of strip lighting, and very opaque paint at that. The darker the shade, the more it masks the fluorescence.

This does not mean that flies with dark-coloured bodies (even black) cannot incorporate D.F.M., as I hope the rest of this chapter will show.

Firstly, we must know what is meant by fluorescence. It is the property of a material to glow when exposed to light rays of a certain type, and to have something more than just plain 'colour'. The effect to the human eye when viewing a fluorescent object is that of a headlamp picking out a reflector at night. The reflector does not just appear red or white, as a piece of painted wood or paper might, but literally glows with colour. Full advantage was taken of this during the war years, when identification armbands of specially treated material were worn by troops engaged in the misty regions of the Aleutians; and shirts and signalling devices on aircraft carriers were also of this new material.

To sum up then, the material at our disposal is a reflector, and when it is exposed to the ultra-violet and other light rays which are always present in daylight (hence D.F.M.), it reflects back its own colour. Under a fluoroscope, or ultra-violet ray lamp, a reel of this material looks as though it is illuminated from inside.

When it was first introduced in the U.S.A., glowing reports were made of its success, and it appeared that many were under the impression that a new wonder material had arrived which would solve all our problems – and provide every novice with the means of gathering huge baskets of fish. Although the material is here to stay, fortunately for the fish, our fishing, and ourselves, baskets still cannot be filled merely by casting in a fly. What we have got, however, is a material which I believe gives the angler a much better advantage in the unequal battle.

Before going on to the uses of D.F.M., one point must be made clear. The material is not active when no light is present. This is usually between one hour before sunrise and one hour after sunset, the ultra-violet light being the last to leave the atmosphere owing to its greater refraction. D.F.M. cannot therefore be expected to attract any better than any other material of similar colouring when night fishing.

In the earliest experiments, D.F.M. was used as a substitute for body materials in general use. If the body of a fly was normally tied green or red, for example, then green or red D.F.M. was used instead of the fur, silk or chenille normally used. As was bound to happen, some fish were caught on the flies, including some that would refuse all other offers at the time. This, of course, aroused enthusiasm at once, but when the same patterns proved utterly worthless at another time it became obvious that all was not well. All idea of a 'wonder' material, irresistible and unfailing, vanished at once. Yet, the spasmodic success indicated that there was something attractive to fish which could be harnessed, perhaps in some other way. It is these 'other ways' which fly tyers want to know about, if only to give them a lead as to which direction in which to experiment.

How to use D.F.M.

1 **Mixing with silks, wools, herls or chenilles** This is the simplest way of incorporating D.F.M. in wet or dry flies, where brilliance is normally part of the pattern.

The normal body material is simply twisted with a piece of D.F.M. of similar texture into a rope and tied in and wound as a body. The amount of brightness is of course governed by the ratio of the mixture, at least two strands of ordinary material being used with one of D.F.M. to keep the brightness reasonable. The effect with this method is that of a brightly-ribbed fly.

A more even mixture may be obtained by unlaying either the wool or silk and really mixing it with fibres of D.F.M., before twisting together. This method is suitable for many flies, particularly salmon and sea-trout patterns. For example a Jock Scott salmon fly can be made very much more attractive with a little D.F.M. added in the following ways. (1) At the tail, a small wisp of fluorescent floss interspersing the Indian crow and golden pheasant crest; (2) in the yellow half of the body, the silk may be wound until the thickness is all but complete, and then one layer of D.F.M. added to give the finishing touch; (3) at the centre, orange, or orange and yellow mixed D.F.M. fibres to replace the toucan veiling. The yellow tag, so common in many salmon fly patterns, may be usefully made of yellow D.F.M.

This mixing in of a small amount of fluorescent material can be used with advantage on many salmon and sea-trout flies, without using too much of the material or making the fly too gaudy. Flies tied in this manner have proved successful, although insufficient evidence is available to prove great superiority over orthodox patterns. We have proved, however, that they give the angler a much better chance in cloudy and swift water. We also know that such flies retain their fresh-tied appearance and brightness even after considerable use, accidents and wear and tear being taken into consideration.

This straightforward method of combining D.F.M. with wool or silk to enliven its appearance can be applied in so many cases and patterns that it would be a formidable task to mention them all. Apart from salmon and sea-trout flies, brown-

trout flies, both wet and dry, may be treated similarly. Any pattern having a wool or
silk body, e.g. Palmer flies, Little Marryat, etc., or any having a bright tag, e.g. Red
Tag, Treacle Parkin, etc., may be improved, in some cases with killing effect, by the
careful addition of D.F.M. blended into the tie. But please note: always the accent
on 'careful'! The secret is to use just enough of the fluorescent materials to tint the
orthodox materials, as it were. To swamp the fly in radiant brilliance does not work
consistently well.

2 Mixing with fur, hair and wool dubbings, and the iridescent effect This is
one of the easiest, and certainly one of the proved effective methods, of using D.F.M.

Furry bodies have always been good on trout, sea-trout and salmon flies, because
under water the fibres float out and give a translucent appearance. Above water, the
light playing on the projecting fibres gives much the same effect. Now, add to these
already excellent materials a little extra sparkle and glow, and there you have one of
the deadliest materials for general use.

Again, the possible combinations are legion, and many have been tried with very
satisfactory results when otherwise poor sport would have been had. The method
here is to cut the D.F.M. (silk or wool according to body texture being used) into
short lengths, comparable with those of the body material, and mix together to obtain
a uniform result. Whatever D.F.M. is added, the result is little different from the
original, but it glows with little points of light wherever the tips of fluorescent strands
show themselves, especially if the D.F.M. is the same colour as the body material.

This method can either be used merely to enrich the colour of the body, or to
obtain iridescent effects. For example, in sea-trout or any other flies having a seal's
fur body, the mixing of a little D.F.M., ratio 1 to 4, with the fur improves the fly,
and the results, considerably. With seal's fur, fluorescent wool, of a similar colour
where possible, is the best material to use.

With other furs, such as hare's ear, D.F.M. can be added in the same way, although
not in the same colour. This is where tinted and iridescent mixtures come in. If one
wishes to strike a particular tone of colour, there is no better way than to choose a
fur near the required tone and add D.F.M. until the exact tone is obtained. The
following is a practical example: a copy of the larva of the ladybird was required, a
beetle-like creature with a dark back and a green-white belly and orange tip. It
sounds complex, but proved easy. The back, of dark green heron herl, was tied in at
the tail ready to lay over beetlewise. The body was made of natural off-white seal's
fur mixed with green to obtain the depth of colour, and then a sprinkling of white and
green fluorescent wool was added. When it was all mixed, it was spread out like a
small cigar and a little orange fluorescent wool was kneaded into one end. A pinch
of the resulting fur, orange tip first, was spun onto the tying silk, and the body wound.
The back was laid over and tied in, and a small Coch-y-Bonddu hackle and black silk
finished the head. This pattern took brace after brace of fish as long as the larvae

fell from the trees onto the river (the Coln) but similar flies with no D.F.M. gave mediocre results. The foregoing dressing explains the principle of tinting existing furs to give better results.

Besides enriching specific colours or using D.F.M. to achieve a particular degree of colour, iridescent effects may be simply obtained with any type of fur. A little pinch of cut D.F.M., of as many colours as desired, is mixed together and then added to some natural fur. By adding or subtracting certain colours the resulting iridescence may be given a bias towards one end of the spectrum or the other. If the D.F.M. is mixed with natural seal's fur, a light grey iridescent fur results. If mixed with hare's ear, a drab brown, and so on with any fur. The result does not look in the least bright, but glows from every point with a fiery pin-prick of colour.

The idea of iridescence is, of course, not new, and trout have long been known to have a fancy for iridescent flies under certain conditions, a fact which was well understood by that wonderful angler and tyer Leonard West, who often used iridescent wings. One has only to examine a few natural insects in a beam of sunlight to appreciate how many of them shine with the colours of the spectrum as the light is refracted from the membranes of their wings and the hairs on their bodies. For this reason iridescent flies, even without D.F.M., give their best results under sunny conditions, but D.F.M. gives the best iridescence of any material.

Now that fluorescent dyes are obtainable, the logical question is, 'Why not dye the furs, instead of mixing them with other fluorescent materials?' Unfortunately, natural furs do not react as well as artificial materials such as nylon, mohair being the only exception. To obtain the best results, therefore, the natural furs should be mixed with the established fluorescent materials.

It must be stressed that there can be no guarantee that this material will solve all our problems and turn every fly into a killer, but it is worth while adding some iridescent mixture to the body of any fly to see if it improves the efficacy of the pattern, particularly in sunshine. It has done so in some cases which have been test-proved and may do so in many more.

3 Mixing with hackle fibres for wings Another method of using D.F.M., with once again unknown limits, is creating iridescent wings with its aid. Flies tied with these wings have brought rewards time and time again under otherwise poor conditions. After considerable trial and error, the best system is this: select some first-quality cock hackles with long, shiny fibres in white, grey, light and dark blue dun and light and dark claret. Lay these out on a flat surface. Take from each one in turn a few fibres (about six to ten with less of the claret than the others) and gather together in a bunch. Mix the fibres up carefully and add short lengths of white, grey, blue and a very little pink D.F.M. floss. This floss is better unlaid so that the fibres will separate and mix with the hackle fibres. When all are mixed well, dip the root end of the bunch in varnish and leave to dry. In this way a few dozen wing sets may be made at a time, and when the varnish is dry they may be stored in a box, and will keep for years.

This method, unlike the one using furs, is simplified by the advent of the new fluorescent dyes. Hackles dye up very well and fluoresce excellently, a large range of delicate olives and duns being available by mixing the dyes appropriately. They can also be dyed in all the eight pastel shades previously mentioned, and blended with the other hackle fibres. I would not, however, suggest that the floss/hackle fibre method be dispensed with entirely, as this has proved to be successful.

When tied into a fly, the wings are treated in the same way as a hackle point or hair wing. Care should be taken to see that if the wing is split to form a double wing, an even distribution of the colours is maintained, particularly of the reds. The tyer may well consider fitting these wings to almost any dry fly. In general, they have proved remarkably successful on imitations of natural insects normally showing iridescence in sunlight, and in particular on the Black Gnat, which dressed in this way has proved the undoing of many brace of 'smutting' fish.

4 Use with horsehair for translucency This is one of the most fascinating, and not the least successful, of the uses of this remarkable substance, and it has been sufficiently tried to show great possibilities.

The aim of many tyers of trout flies has been to obtain natural translucency, and horsehair was one of the mediums used to produce it. Not only will D.F.M. with horsehair produce translucency, but such a good degree of it as to equal that of the natural insect in many cases, despite the ever-present hook shank. The method is simply to use D.F.M. floss wound along the hook shank as a base over which horsehair is then wound, in either a single or double layer. The whole is then lightly varnished with very thin, clear varnish. The colour of the body is graded and controlled either by clear hair over coloured D.F.M., or coloured hair over white D.F.M., or a combination of colours in both. The horsehair/floss combination may be varied to obtain a variety of shades of olive, such as clear hair over yellow floss, or olive hair over white floss, and so on. The reason for the translucency is that the light passing through the hair is reflected back by the fluorescent core, instead of striking the opaque hook shank, giving the illusion that the whole is a semi-clear homogeneous substance. These flies when finished are amazingly faithful copies of the natural, and are deadly when fished during a rise. Experiments have shown that imitations tied with horsehair and D.F.M. which look good copies of the natural insect to the tyer, will almost certainly look so to the fish. One tip to remember with this method is to use horsehair that is quite clear before dyeing, and not to dye it too deeply.

Just one last word of advice: do not hesitate to use even the most fantastic combinations of D.F.M., do not expect great results, but do not be surprised if you get them.

Some successful experiments were carried out by that well-known angler Gordon Hay. He incorporated D.F.M. to give more lifelike brilliance to the bodies of his flies, and to help produce a greater amount of translucent light. He also confirmed the theory that flies tied with a proportion of D.F.M. were more effective on dull days, or at dawn or dusk.

The methods used by Hay, and the patterns he described, are well worth studying.

One of his most successful patterns (over four seasons) was a Partridge and Red. This was tied on long-shanked up-eyed hooks size 14-11, with a wool-mix body, three turns of orange D.F.M. as a tag and a brown partridge hackle. Red tying silk was used throughout. The wool-mix for the body was made up of equal lengths of dark brown and fawn ordinary, skein wool, mixed with similar lengths of orange and pink D.F.M. wool. All the lengths must be thoroughly teased out before mixing, and one of the best ways to do this is to hold the wool firmly in one hand, take a pair of tweezers in the other, grip the wool firmly about $\frac{1}{2}$ in. from its loose end and draw the tweezers along the wool. This will produce a fluffy end to the wool which can be cut off, and the process can be repeated until the whole length of the wool has been treated. To mix the four shades of wool thoroughly, hold them all in the left hand and tear out a pinch at a time, pulling all four colours with each pinch. Let the pinches form a little pile on the table until all the wool has been teased out, and repeat the process until an even mix has been obtained.

The orange D.F.M. floss for the tag is tied in just above the point of the long-shanked hook, three turns to the rear, and then back over itself. Hold the floss taut when tying it off, as it has a tendency to slip. The wool-mix is now spun very lightly onto the tying silk, tapering it off so that there is practically none where the silk meets the hook. Wind along the shank of the hook to form a tapering body, slim throughout, but with a thickening at the thorax. Now tie in the partridge hackle, and secure. Next, take the hackle between the finger and thumb of the left hand, and draw all the fibres upwards and backwards towards the bend of the hook. Hold in this position and secure with a few turns of the tying silk, so that all the fibres are set above the hook. Black cellulose varnish finishes the head.

The hackle fibres for these flies should be short and need not be longer than the distance from the head of the fly to the point of the hook. Rib with fine gold wire for lake use.

Another successful pattern, originally tied for evening use, is the Twilight Grey. Captain J. Hughes Parry, in August 1951, took eight fish, out of a total catch of ten, on this fly, and dressed on a No. 5 long-shank hook; he also took a $2\frac{1}{2}$ lb sea-trout, and a $1\frac{1}{4}$ lb brown, when no other flies would move a fish. Dressed on sizes 16-14 and 13 it has taken many trout from lake and river. The dressing is:

Hackle: Grizzle (Plymouth Rock) cock
Body: Grey wool-mix
Tying silk: Grey or olive

The wool-mix is made up of a length of medium grey tapestry wool, and a length of white fluorescent wool only one-third as long as the grey wool. The two should be thoroughly mixed as for the Partridge and Red. Grey fluorescent wool can also be used to vary the shade of the body. The wool-mix should be very thin and tapering when spun onto the tying silk, and a tapering body should be formed – slightly thicker at the thorax.

Two or three turns of hackle are sufficient for wet flies, but more may be added if they are to be used dry. For sea-trout, No. 5 long-shank hooks are recommended, with a slightly longer hackle for the extra length of hook.

The third dressing given by Mr Hay is the ever-popular Black Gnat, tied both wet and dry. A stiff, black cock hackle is used for the dry pattern, and a starling hackle for the wet, and they are tied on sizes 16–14.

The tying silk is black, of course, and this is whipped from the eye towards the bend of the hook. The stem of the hackle is then placed on these turns, and the silk whipped back from the eye, leaving enough space in front for the hackle to be wound. The silk is then wound back towards the bend, finishing opposite the point. At this stage a piece of white D.F.M. floss is tied in. Secure it firmly and then take two turns towards the bend, and then two or three back to cover the first two, so as to form a small pea about the size of a pin-head. Keep the floss as tight as possible. Tie in the waste end of the floss with the tying silk and cut off. Now take two turns of the tying silk over the floss, each turn lying next to its neighbour, so as to form a slight bulge towards the tail. Next whip back over all the tying silk up to the point required for winding the hackle. Wind the hackle and tie in its tip, cut off any surplus and seal off the head with black cellulose varnish.

The last dressing is a variation of the Coch-y-Bonddu. When the tying silk is wound down to the bend for tying in the peacock herl body, a small loop of white D.F.M. floss is first tied in. The loop is then cut and teased out with the tying silk to form a small, fluffy tassel, which is trimmed with the scissors so that only about one-sixteenth of an inch projects from the herl body. Mr Hay's preference was for a dark red game cock's hackle in place of the more usual red/black, but only because it was more successful on the particular waters he fished. A fine gold tinsel rib was found to be an asset on cold dull days.

I had a great deal of correspondence at one time with the late William Bannerman, an expert fisherman and fly tyer, of Buckle, Banffshire, and he was always a valuable source of information on lesser-known trout and salmon patterns.

He devoted a lot of time to experiments with fluorescent material, and I could not do better than quote his conclusions.

I have done quite a bit of experimenting with D.F.M. this season, and although disappointed with the length of time taken to try out the idea, I am quite pleased with some of the results. Some of the experiments proved most successful, but there still remains the doubt that the originals may have done quite as well under the same circumstances. Following are some of the new ideas, at least original in my case, which were tried out and in my opinion were an improvement on the standard pattern.

Floss silks rolled in chopped D.F.M. of various colours, and then wound on the hook-shank before building the bodies called for in the pattern. This was very good on such patterns as Coch-y-Bonddu and Rough Olive, and patterns calling for seal's fur and other dubbings.

Single strands of D.F.M. floss dividing and shading quill bodies.

Single strands ribbed the same as tinsel.

Hair and spade hackle wings with a minute quantity of D.F.M. floss strands to give flash.

A single strand of blue floss twisted round the ribbing tinsel on such flies as the Teal Blue and Silver. This method can be applied to any fly with a silver body.

The only conclusions I would stick my neck out for are:

That combined with horsehair translucency can be obtained to a satisfactory degree.

That floss silks rolled in chopped D.F.M. can obtain many combinations which seem attractive to fish.

That tails of yellow D.F.M. shading short tails of orange D.F.M. are at least as successful if not more so than standard tails.

That D.F.M. should be used more sparingly in low clear water than in deep coloured water.

In case you are interested in sea and bait fishing, I must tell you about the uses of D.F.M. with these.

Sea flies. Use as with ordinary flies.

Minnows, especially wooden devons in the spring, lend themselves to use with D.F.M., the most successful being single strands of D.F.M. laid parallel along the belly on wet varnish, and then thoroughly re-varnished with clear Cellire. In some cases the strands were stiffened with varnish and fixed to extend beyond the minnow body and almost covering the treble hook.

Metal sea baits. The most easily worked, of course, are the lead type. Holes are bored through the flat sides of the bait, and D.F.M. floss threaded in and out. Or the holes can be filled with short lengths of the floss and wool, which are then cut quite close to the body. In both systems the bodies are varnished after the D.F.M. has been added. Many variations can be made, the best I found being one with spots of red or blue.

Sea fishing may well provide a useful field for this type of experiment. My only regret is that I have neither the time or health to experiment with this type of material as much as it deserves.

Since this was written many new patterns have been evolved which use P.V.C. strip, and if fluorescent floss or wool is first wound under this it can give a very interesting translucent effect. One pattern in particular is the Polystickle, when one can reproduce the 'gut' of the fry with a few turns of orange or scarlet fluorescent wool or silk before winding the P.V.C. strip.

A fluorescence detector

Although the best test for fluorescent fly-tying materials is to use them when fishing, it is, of course, desirable to know the amount of fluorescence present in the fly to be used, or the amount of fluorescence being given off by the material which is to go into the fly.

The normal method is to use a quartz mercury vapour lamp, with the visible light screened by a special nickel glass filter, but this is an expense to which few fly tyers are prepared to go. It is, however, possible to use the ultra-violet light present in sunlight to operate a simple detector, an example of which is illustrated below. It is a small wooden box with a sliding lid, the inside of which is blackened with indian ink. A hole is cut in the lid, which takes a piece of special nickel glass to form a screen 2×2 in.

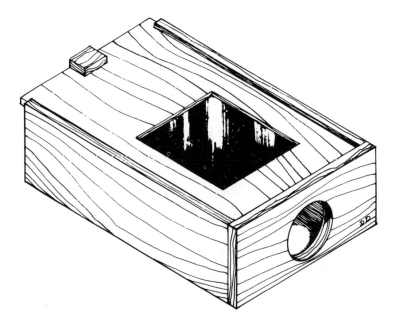

The material or flies to be tested are put into the box, and with the eye close to the hole in front of the box to exclude all light, allow sunlight to fall on the screen. Artificial light does not produce much fluorescence, but there will be enough for demonstration purposes. Incandescent electric light is the best source, should there be no sunlight.

Some information on the lasting powers of fluorescent materials will be helpful. Tests were carried out over nine weeks June/July 1954, which, incidentally, was the wettest summer for half a century.

D.F.M. exposed to daylight only was still as good as ever after twelve months, and flies used throughout the season still reacted as well as when they were first tied.

The continuous exposure test began on 1 June, and a complete range of D.F.M. was exposed to the elements (sun, wind, rain) with the object of seeing just how much they would stand.

During the month of June there was 3 in. of rain and an average $5\frac{1}{2}$ hours sunshine per day. Coupled with the high winds, these conditions were very severe, but they made only a small impression on the D.F.M. There was very little fading either in the actual colours of the materials or in the fluorescence, which was very encouraging, as these conditions must have been as severe, if not more so, than any fly would normally have to contend with.

The tests were carried on into July with the same materials, and during that month there was a further $2\frac{1}{2}$ in. of rain and an average of $4\frac{1}{2}$ hours of sunshine per day. By the end of the month most of the materials had begun to wilt, and the degree of deterioration was carefully noted. It should be borne in mind that any dyed material would have faded after two months' exposure to such conditions, and also that for maximum fluorescence D.F.M. is only dyed in light pastel shades.

The results of the test are shown in the table on page 108.

Results at the end of continuous exposure test on D.F.M. materials
(9 weeks – June/July 1954)
Conditions: heavy rail (5·44 inches) wind and bright sunshine (297·4 hours)

	HACKLES	WOOL	CHENILLE	FLOSS
WHITE	Complete loss of fluorescence	Complete loss of fluorescence	Complete loss of fluorescence	Complete loss of fluorescence
BLUE	Complete fading and loss of fluorescence	Some fading and complete loss of fluorescence	Some fading and complete loss of fluorescence	Complete fading and loss of fluorescence
GREY	Complete fading and loss of fluorescence	Some fading and complete loss of fluorescence	Some fading and complete loss of fluorescence	Complete fading and loss of fluorescence
LIME	Severe fading, but fairly good fluorescence	Some fading and slight loss of fluorescence	Some fading and slight loss of fluorescence	Severe fading (see note regarding fluorescence)
YELLOW	Severe fading, but fairly good fluorescence	Slight fading, but fairly good fluorescence	Slight fading, but fairly good fluorescence	Severe fading (see note regarding fluorescence)
ORANGE	Slight fading, but fair fluorescence	Slight fading, but fair fluorescence	Slight fading, but fair fluorescence	Severe fading (see note regarding fluorescence)
SCARLET	Very little fading and very good fluorescence	Slight fading, but good fluorescence	Slight fading, but very good fluorescence	Severe fading (see note regarding fluorescence)
PINK	Severe fading, but quite fair fluorescence	Slight fading, but fair fluorescence	Slight fading and slight loss of fluorescence	Severe fading (see note regarding fluorescence)

Note : Severest loss of colour was found in the floss, and colours which retained fluorescence in this material were dominated by yellow.

15

Varnishes and wax

The main function of varnish is to protect the finishing winds of the tying silk, but it has a secondary role in that it can be used decoratively as well. White, yellow and red on black will make 'eyes' for streamer flies, as well as being used for the distinctive colouring of most salmon fly heads.

It can also strengthen the bodies of flies if delicate materials such as ostrich herl and peacock herl are being used, and it will give added life to deer hair bodied flies. To achieve this, thin, clear varnish should be applied to the hook shank before the materials are wound on.

Most varnishes are of the cellulose variety, and can be obtained in a variety of colours. If you are ever caught out by having none available, ordinary nail varnish will do. All these varnishes tend to thicken with the passage of time, especially if lids are left off too long, but thinners are available for the cellulose variety.

Another hard-setting varnish which has come into use in recent years is of the

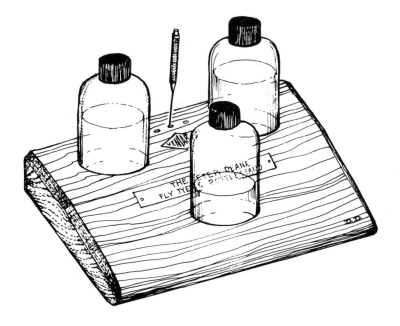

polyurethane group, marketed under the names of Venglaze and Vycoat. These cannot be thinned once they start to harden, so you should pour out a small amount for immediate use, and replace the lid tightly on the main supply as quickly as possible.

Fly-tying wax is obtainable from all dealers in fly-tying materials, and is usually in the form of a specially prepared cake. It remains fairly hard when not in use, but can be softened rapidly either in the hand, or by pulling the tying silk through it very quickly. This creates friction, which melts the wax as the silk passes through it. Once again, if you are caught short there is a substitute in the old-fashioned wax used by shoe menders, still referred to as cobbler's wax.

Wax can also be obtained in liquid form, when it is applied with a dubbing needle, and many tackle firms list a pre-waxed tying thread.

Most varnishes, their thinners, and liquid wax are bought in small bottles, and knocking one over can have disastrous results. To avoid this, a neat bottle stand was designed by Mr Peter Deane, the well-known professional fly dresser, and an illustration of this is shown on page 109.

16

Storing and preserving materials, and the workbench

The best method for storing one's materials, if funds will allow, is a specially designed cabinet with sectioned drawers to take all the tools, accessories and feathers.

In addition to my own cabinet I have a portable plastic case, designed specifically for fly-tying materials by The Efgee Co. of London. I have no doubt that some of the other tackle boxes one sees advertised regularly could be converted.

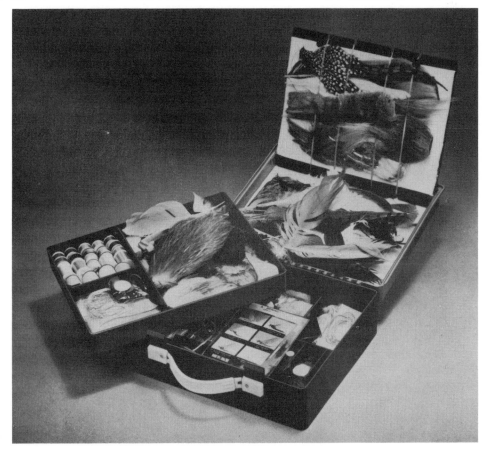

Whatever method is used for storing, all compartments, boxes and packets should be liberally sprinkled with some form of parasite deterrent, especially to prevent attack by moth grubs. The old stand-by is flake carbon (or napthalene), but there are now one or two chemical preparations on the market which are most efficacious.

I am indebted to Mr Tom Green, of Cupar, Scotland, who has used his experience as a time-and-motion study expert to devise an ideal layout for fly tying. This uses the minimum amount of space to give the maximum amount of comfort and economy of time.

We have all experienced the exasperation of losing tools or odd items of material while tying a fly, and also the calumny heaped upon us, usually by the distaff side of our families, for the messiness usually associated with home fly tying.

Mr Green's suggestions should go a long way towards dealing with these disadvantages, and he says: 'The following is an appraisal of the fly-tying area, using basic work-study techniques, which it is hoped will present a logical system of working.'

It will be seen that the major item shown in Donald Downs' illustrations is the material cabinet. In my opinion, one of these is essential for home tying (and I am speaking from experience) and the simple one shown, or something like it, should either be available or within the capabilities of most of us to make, whether a dedicated handyman or not. Donald has a very good example, which has all his materials in plastic boxes, a vice, tools and a battery operated table lamp, all contained within a wooden box, the lid of which drops down to form the workbench.

To see how the layout works, let us take a simple fly such as the Teal Blue and Silver, for which we would expect to have the following tools and materials to hand: vice, hackle pliers, scissors, dubbing needle, whip finish tool, hook, tying silk, wax, tippet fibres for the tail, body tinsel, blue hackle, teal flank for wings, and varnish for the head. In all, thirteen items.

The problem is to arrange the items in a manner that will enable them to be brought together with the least effort.

Considering first the capabilities of the tyer's body, one can see from Fig. 1 the areas covered by the hands when the arms are extended, and also when the arms remain bent. To avoid any strain, materials and tools should be placed in this latter area, and if they are arranged in curves this will encourage curved movements of the hands. These factors produce a layout as shown in Fig. 2.

The tools should be kept at a fixed point, and this is shown at **c** in the sketch. A wooden block with pot magnets inserted might be used to good advantage, since this allows the tools to be fixed without the fussiness of clips, hooks or other aids. Item **d** represents a foam pad for hooks, and **c** is the varnish holder on which the block of wax can also be placed. Many tyers prefer to varnish fly heads as a final operation after all the flies have been tied, in which case the varnishes can be left out of the layout.

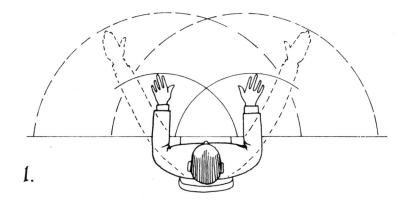

1.

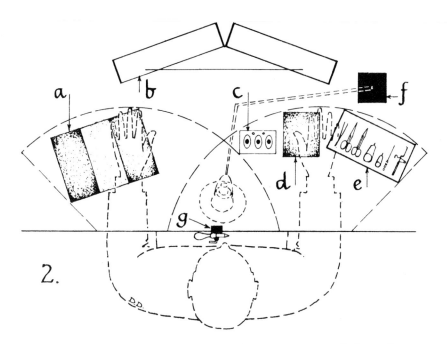

2.

a. Foam pads.
   (materials)

b. Storage Cabinet.

c. Varnishes.

d. Foam pad.
   (hooks)

e. Tools.   f. Lamp   g. Vice.

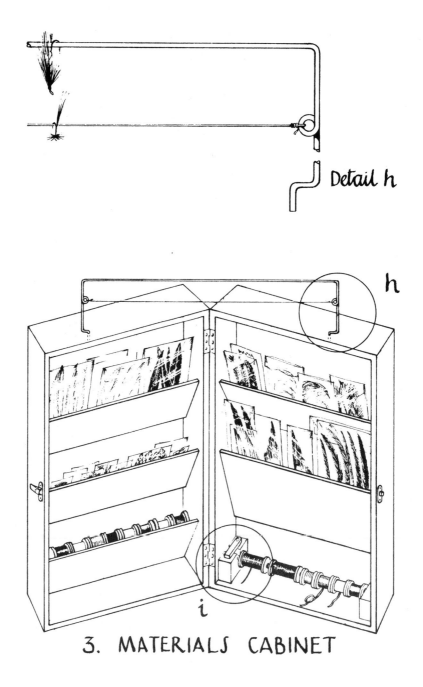

Detail h

h

i

3. MATERIALS CABINET

The lamp shown at **f** is of the Anglepoise type, and care should be taken to make sure that direct glare is avoided. For my own use, I have a similar type of lamp with the added advantage of a 4 in. square magnifying glass which can be folded down between the face and the jaws of the vice when I am tying very small flies, or wish to make a close inspection of flies or material.

The best position for the vice would appear to be at **g**, as shown, since from time to time various materials may dangle from it, and the fact that it protrudes beyond the edge of the working surface makes this possible. Any waste material will, of course, drop onto the floor or the tyer's lap, which gives an opportunity of using a rubbish tray or apron, thus reducing the waste of time and the inconvenience of scrabbling on the floor picking up the waste pieces.

This description represents a layout for 'immediate' materials, but secondary items can be stored in a reasonably accessible area in the simple materials cabinet illustrated. This prototype was manufactured from a disused cutlery box, and with a little thought it can be arranged to store all the tools used also.

The sketch of the cabinet (Fig. 3) is self-explanatory, with details as follows: **h** is a varnish drying rail for larger flies, made from a piece of $\frac{3}{32}$ in. diam. wire – from a metal coathanger, in fact. A piece of wire or monofilament (my own choice) may also be strung between the uprights for smaller flies, care being taken that a bow-string effect is not created – a heavy hand could cause a chaotic flight of completed flies in all directions. The rail serves a dual purpose in that it also acts as a 'steady' for the partially opened cabinet. Detail **i** shows a simple method of storing spools of tinsels and body silks.

Tying silks are kept in the lower left-hand compartment of the box, each spool being mounted on a bobbin holder. They are placed in the sloping compartment with the spool at the top, so that any required colour can be selected immediately.

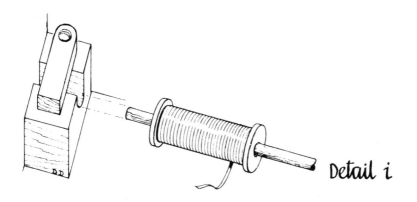

Detail i

Polystyrene foam pads are used for the materials, and these should be of dark and light colours, as shown at **a** in Fig. 2. Light-coloured materials should be placed on the dark pads, and dark ones on the light pads, of course, as shown above. Hackles, wing feathers, tails etc., should be selected and prepared before starting the tying operations, since selecting them during the actual tying would upset the rhythm. These items should be laid out on the foam pads. Floss body silks and tinsels can be cut into lengths varying from 4 in. to 6 in., according to the size of the fly to be tied. The 'give' in the foam pads will be seen to be a great help when picking up the individual items, making the use of tweezers unnecessary.

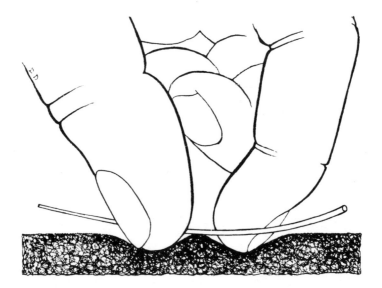

I would like to add a small contribution of my own, and it is remotely connected with the ideas suggested by Mr Green. It concerns the varnishing of heads. I know it is normal practice to use a dubbing needle for this, but no matter how meticulously this is wiped after use, eventually there is a build-up of hardened varnish some way up the point, which has to be cleaned off. I never use a needle for this purpose, preferring to use the quills of some of the feathers in continual use. These can be quills from the flight feathers of the starling's wing, the blue-black mallard wing quills, brown mallard shoulder feathers, or any quills of a similar size. When the feather fibres have been stripped from the quills (both sides) for winging, I save half a dozen or so and strip them completely to within $\frac{1}{8}-\frac{1}{4}$ in. of the tip of the quill, any remaining fibres being snipped off by cutting off the tip of the quill. I then use these quills to apply the varnish to the heads of my flies. Although the fibres have been stripped off cleanly, the quills themselves have a certain amount of roughness, which retains the bead of varnish, so that it does not run off the point, as usually happens when the needle applicator is used. By dipping just $\frac{1}{16}-\frac{1}{8}$ in. of the quill into the varnish bottle, enough varnish is picked up to finish off two or three flies, and when the tying session is over the quills can be discarded with the rest of the rubbish.

17

Preparing golden pheasant crests for tying in

These feathers, when on the living bird, are a perfect shape for putting on a salmon fly, but during the drying and storing of the skins many of the crests get twisted out of shape. It is logical to assume, therefore, that if one form of treatment will put the feathers out of shape, another will restore them.

Moistening them and placing them in the curve of a wine glass is one method frequently advocated, but this limits the shapes one can achieve and does not always remove the twist. The best method I know is to moisten them thoroughly and then lay them on their sides, on a smooth surface, in the shape you wish them to be. I use part of a linoleum-covered workbench myself, and, provided one knows that the feathers are clean, saliva is the best moistener.

The feathers must be made very wet, and the required shape is given to them with the finger-tips. Any shape can be achieved, from a dead straight line to a half-circle, or the end of the crest can be turned down sharply, so that it curves to meet the tail of the fly in a pleasing manner.

The crests should be left on the flat surface until they are quite dry, otherwise the shape is not maintained. On removal, it will be seen that all the fibres of the crest are clinging together, and to bring it back to its natural state I use a stiffish fibred brush, of the type normally used to clean typewriter keys. This brushing will not remove the shape, especially if the crests are allowed to stand for a good length of time before being picked up. I like to leave mine for twenty-four hours.

The next step is to remove the unwanted fibres from the butt end of the crest, leaving it the right length for the fly to be tied. The stripped butt is then flattened between the thumbnail and the ball of the first finger, and the soaking makes the quill more amenable to this treatment.

One very good point with this method is that as the crest has lain on its side during the shaping process, the curve is always in an exactly flat plane, with all twist removed. Therefore, when it is placed over the wing, the flattened quill can be tied in at once, without being manipulated, so that the crest will envelop the wing properly.

It is always a good idea to select a crest about $\frac{1}{2}$ in. longer than the wing to be covered, as this makes it easier for the stripped and flattened butt to be tied in.

Crests for tails can be treated in the same manner, again using one longer than is strictly necessary, so that only the butt is tied in and none of the fibres. This prevents the latter splaying out in all directions.

The foregoing instructions may seem rather long-drawn-out, but the actual procedure is very simple and will give that extra 'finish' which is the hallmark of a well-tied fly.

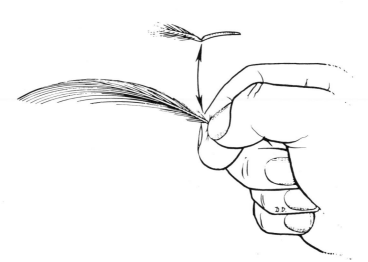

18

Doubling hackles

There are several methods of turning back the fibres of hackles, known to us all through various books of instruction, but I will keep to what I think is the simplest. This involves the use of a spare hook and the tying vice and hackle pliers.

The hackle to be doubled is tied onto the hook by its tip or butt, and then held vertically by the hackle pliers. The fibres are then stroked to the left, best side outside, until the necessary 'V' sectional appearance is achieved. It is as simple as that. I advise doubling the hackles on a spare hook, because if one strokes the fibres a little too vigorously the hackle may be pulled from the hook, and this would be a calamity if a body hackle was involved as the body of the fly would have to be unwound and the hackle tied in afresh. This is not as important, of course, if it is a throat hackle. Also, using this method, several hackles may be prepared and then put aside until they are needed. The illustrations may be of some help, Figs. 1, 2 and 3 showing how the hackle is tied in and treated.

Note that the hackle is tied in close to the body and then wound towards the eye of the hook (Fig. 4).

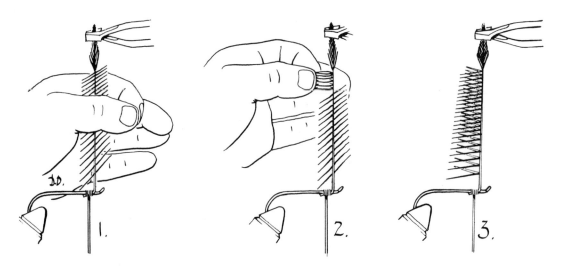

When winding a body hackle, it is important to make sure that the hackle stalk is not twisted in any way, otherwise the 'doubling' is nullified. It also helps if the fibres are stroked back towards the tail during the winding. Make sure that every turn of the hackle is close up against its companion turn of ribbing tinsel, as this not only protects the hackle stalk, but also keeps the doubled hackle fibres in position (Fig. 5). Fig. 6 shows both doubled body hackles and throat hackles on a fly which is now ready for winging.

Another method of doubling was given to me by Jimmy Younger, whose family have been well known in Scottish fly tying and fly fishing for several generations. The hackle pliers gripping the hackle to be doubled are held in the hand, as shown in Figs. 1, 2 and 3 on page 122.

If doubling hackles still presents some difficulty, the following method of making 'false' hackles may give better results. It is another one of the ideas sent to me by the late Captain the Hon. R. Coke, and although it is not a new idea, as he freely admitted, he considered it to be one not used generally enough.

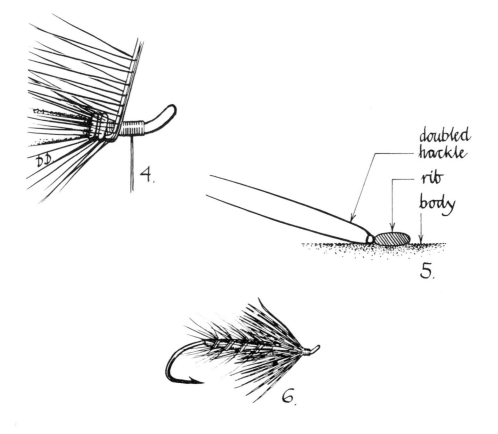

doubled
hackle
rib
body

4.

5.

6.

'False' hackles consist of a bunch of fibres torn from a feather and tied in at the throat in very much the same way as one would tie in a wing. With this method, such difficult feathers as blue jay can be used without the bother of splitting the quill, and the inevitable resulting breakages, giving greater economy and also reducing bulk at the head of the fly. Ordinary poultry hackles which are too large for normal use can also be used on flies of any size. The procedure is as follows.

The fly is tied to the stage at which it is necessary to add the throat hackle, and the tying silk is anchored with a half-hitch. The hook is then taken from the vice and put back upside down. The feather to be used as a hackle is selected, and its fibres are then pulled down to stand out at right-angles to the stem. Tear off a good bunch of the fibres, keeping their tips in line as much as possible. These fibres are now tied in on top of the hook shank (this is underneath, of course, as the hook is upside down), using the normal winging method of the loop over the finger and thumb of the left hand. To spread the fibres over the whole area of the throat, it is a good idea to place

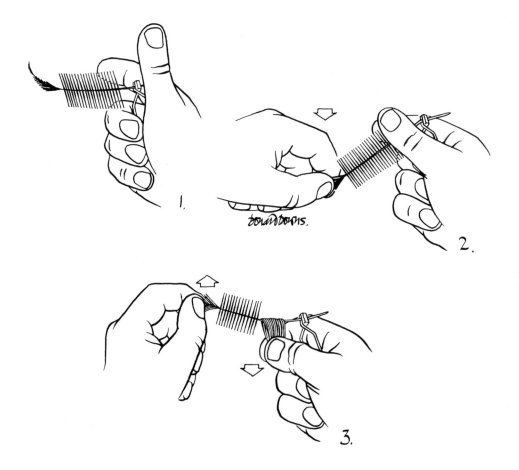

the fibres rather more to the side of the hook facing you, so that when the silk is drawn tight the fibres are pulled over to the far side. In other words, although we are using the winging method to tie in the fibres, we should forget about all the principles we have learned for bringing feather fibres down one on top of the other, but try to produce a split 'wing'.

After one turn of the tying silk has been taken, it should be put in the retaining button or hackle pliers (if not weighted with a bobbin holder), and the fibres should be separated and adjusted with a dubbing needle or stiletto. One bunch of fibres is usually enough, but on larger flies two small additional bunches can be tied in, one on either side of the original one.

This process may sound involved, but in practice it is very simple. Moreover, when the hook is once again reversed it will be found that there is practically no 'hump' to be levelled off before the wings are tied in, which means that a small head results and the wings lie low over the body.

Many feathers other than jay can be tied in by this method to give pleasing results. Partridge body feathers, heron, guinea fowl (gallena) all lend themselves to it, and so the necessity of doubling them is avoided. It can only be applied to throat hackles, of course, as body hackles must still be wound on the stem.

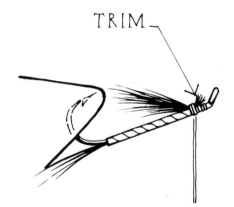

TRIM

19

Stiffening dry-fly hackles

Still on the subject of hackles, Captain Coke also used the following method of stiffening his dry-fly hackles – an idea born of the scarcity of the good quality hackles required to keep flies afloat. It is this: after completing the fly to the stage at which the hackle is required, select a large hackle of the same colour and cut off about 1 in. from the tip. This is the best part to use, as any web which there may be in the feather is much less apparent at its extreme tip. Stroke the fibres to right-angles with the stem and clip them to about ⅛ in. on either side of the stem. The length varies according to the size of fly, of course, but in this instance we are left with a hackle 1 in. long with a width of ¼ in. along its entire length.

This hackle is now tied in at the shoulder of the fly, and one, or at the most two, turns taken around the hook shank and finished off. The ordinary hackle is then selected and tied in and wound behind and in front of the cut hackle, and the fly finished off in the usual way.

The stiff, short fibres of the cut hackle act as stiffeners to the weaker fibres of the ordinary hackle, and are quite invisible if the job is done properly. A fly tied in this manner works best in rough water, where it is most important to have one which cocks and floats well.

Incidentally, this two-hackle principle is used for the Dr Baigent Refracta dry flies, the difference being that instead of the long-fibred hackle being cut short it is left long, the effective hackle making the legs forming the centre of the hackle. By doing this, Dr Baigent claimed that the surface of the water was disturbed by the fibres of the long hackle, altering the refraction and giving a more natural look to the artificial from the fish's point of view.

The heavy hackling required to float dapping flies, through the air as well as on the surface of the water, requires little explanation, so I have provided no drawings for this. The only point to remember is that instead of one single hackle being tied in and wound, two or three are tied in together and wound at the same time as though they were a single hackle. This produces the thick 'bushy' effect which is the main characteristic of dapping flies.

20

Skinning a chicken

With modern methods of breeding and rearing poultry, one does not often get hold of a rooster or rare-coloured hen bird. It does happen sometimes, however, that someone living near, or knowing, a game-bird breeder or owner of a run of free-range chickens, gets the offer of a prime old cock bird. To see its plumage go to waste in these days of hackle shortages would be almost criminal, so I hope these brief instructions on how to skin the bird will prompt the sudden owner of a fine Coch-y-Bonddu or Plymouth Rock Cock (amongst others) to rescue and preserve the feathers for future use.

For the squeamish, a dead bird is preferable of course, but if you have to kill it yourself, a swift blow with an iron bar or the back of an axe just where the head meets the neck will do. At the back of course. This should make a clean break in the neck, killing the bird instantly.

The skinning is carried out as follows. Using a thin-bladed knife, make an incision in the breast just below the cape area. Only the skin should be penetrated, not the meat. When you have checked that the incision is correctly made, run the blade up through the skin to the base of the head, or to where the bird's chin would be if it had one. It should now be possible to start peeling the sides of the cut away from the skin, although a little help from your knife may be necessary. When you have made sure that everything is in order, and that the initial incision was the right length (i.e. not too short), make a cut around the base of the cape, from the underside of the skin. This will free all the skin at the base, so it should now be possible to pull the whole cape off the bird by pulling upwards towards the head. Make sure the small hackles at the top of the head come away too, and then cut the cape off and lay it on one side.

Garden shears or secateurs can be used to cut the wings from the body, and we should next remove the saddle. This is on the back of the bird, and contains the spade feathers which are useful for tails and Spiders, and along its edges are the long, slender hackles used on many streamer patterns.

To remove the saddle, grasp a fold of skin where the cape was removed, make an incision to free it from the flesh and, still using your knife as necessary, work around to each side of the area which contains the saddle. Once you have cleared one side, it becomes quite easy to slice and pull the rest of it away from the bird.

The tail feathers can be cut off in the same way as the wings if you consider them usable, but it is not often that there is a use for any other feathers on the body.

The next stage of the proceedings is to preserve and protect the skins. A wash in a mild detergent such as Venpol will see off any parasites that may be present, and there are not many birds or animals that do not have them. This will also clean the feathers, and remove any traces of blood which may have stained them. When clean, lay them on several thicknesses of newspaper to dry – skin downwards. It does not matter if some of the newspaper sticks to the skin during the drying process, and although your cape will look a 'right mess' after it has been washed, once the drying process starts, the feathers will soon start to reassume their natural glossiness. It helps to fluff the hackle in a warm atmosphere. Beating it gently against one hand as the drying process advances will help this fluffing process. As the skin dries it may start to curl up at the edges, so to overcome this, lay the cape skin down again on a newspaper with another one on top. This will help retain the shape and is best carried out whilst the skin is still slightly damp. The top newspaper should be removed after a day or so in order for the full drying process to take place. If the fully-dried cape ends up with a slight curve, or 'dishing', this is not a disadvantage, and is in fact a help when it comes to extracting the hackles. Any bent or twisted feathers can be straightened by holding the part of the cape concerned in the steam from a kettle – the oldest-known 'beautifier' of all feathers.

Notes on storing and preserving feathers will be found in chapter 16, and, with the hackle skin, a little borax rubbed into it before it is dry, will prevent flies or other parasites from laying their eggs in it, or stop the hatching of any that may be there already.

21

Afterthoughts

Although this is not a book of fly-dressing instruction, there are one or two categories of material which should receive special attention. One of these is seal and other furs, and involves the blending of various colours, and storing.

It is often necessary, to achieve some particular shade, to mix two or more furs together. This mostly happens when some particular shade of olive is required, and if one has two or three packets of dyed olive, ranging from light to dark, many variations can be produced.

These can also be tinted further with browns, reds, orange, and so on, if warmer shades are required, and a very good fiery brown can be produced by mixing chocolate, red and orange.

It will, of course, be apparent that there is no limit to the colours one can achieve.

The secret of success is to do only a little at a time. It is also important that the correct ratio of ingredients should be kept. A small portion of the smallest ingredient, about the size of a pea, should be selected, and teased out to make as large a bulk as possible, so that it becomes more like a piece of fluff. The correct proportion of the next ingredient should be treated in the same manner. The two heaps of dubbing, when sufficiently opened out, should then be placed one on top of the other, and thoroughly mixed together by breaking and refolding until a more or less uniform colour is obtained.

When the pile is well mixed, small sections should be broken off and treated as was the pea-sized portion at the beginning. These should be mixed individually until the whole pile has been treated, and then all the separate piles of 'fluff' mixed together again.

In this way it is possible to obtain one uniform colour, provided that clashing colours are not used, of course. I doubt very much if a good grey could be obtained by trying to mix a black and a white. It is, however, possible to blend suitable colours to achieve a uniform shade.

When it is necessary to blend fluorescent material into a dubbing, it is better to use a wool rather than a floss. The wool should be cut in strips of about $\frac{3}{4}$ in., and then teased out into a very fine fluff. In this form it is very easy to mix into the main dubbing.

It often happens that, when one comes to the actual mixing, the staple of one ingredient is found to be longer than the other. While it will not altogether prevent the mixing of the two ingredients, it is much easier to mix them if the fibres of each are more or less the same length. Therefore, the dubbing with the longer fibres should be cut across several times with a pair of sharp scissors until it is reduced to the same consistency as the other fur to be mixed.

Loose dubbing left on the fly-tying bench can easily be blown away or get mixed up with other materials unless stored properly, although it should still be readily available.

The best method, and the most usual, is a flat wooden or strong cardboard box with circular holes cut in the top about $\frac{1}{2}$–$\frac{3}{4}$ in. in diameter. The holes should be in rows with about $\frac{1}{2}$ in. between them. All one has to do then is push a different colour of fur into each hole, putting in sufficient fur to just 'hump' above the level of the hole. As one picks off the small quantities used each time, the natural springiness of the fur will keep the hump just above the surface. The fur should be picked up with tweezers each time, to make sure that only a little is taken.

If one wishes to leave the furs in the packets in which they are purchased (usually cellophane envelopes), these should be left sealed and just a small triangle cut off one corner. The springiness of the fur will push a small amount through the gap made, and it can be used without distributing most of it around the bench.

Another very good method of mixing furs is to place them together in a jar of water, and then shake the jar rapidly. The resulting 'mess' of fur is squeezed as dry as possible, and left on a sheet of newspaper to dry out completely. One will have to wait longer for the fur when using this method, but it is less tedious than mixing by hand, and does ensure a well-balanced product.

Making dubbing bodies

I was shown the following method by a professional tyer who gave me my first instruction in tying many years ago, and I have yet to see a better one either for quickness in application or durability in use.

We all must have seen illustrations of dubbing spiralled round the tying silk, but this is not good enough if the fur is to stay on during use. It must completely enclose the tying silk, as does the rubber casing on a piece of electrical flex.

There are a number of important points to remember during the spinning of the fur onto the silk.

1 See that the tying silk is well waxed.
2 Use only a small amount of the fur at a time, spread out to cover as large an area of the thumb as possible.
3 Do *not* roll the silk backwards and forwards on the thumb, but roll it in one direction only.
4 Keep the tying silk taut at all times.

The procedure is as follows: hold the tying silk taut in the right hand, at right-angles to the hook and pulling it towards the body. Select a minute pinch of the fur and spread it on the ball of the left forefinger or thumb, whichever you find easiest. If the fur looks more like an almost invisible mist than a bunch of fibres so much the better, especially for small trout flies. Now bring the taut silk down on the forefinger, as shown in Fig. 1. Lower the thumb of the left hand onto the forefinger and roll the silk *and* the fur in a clockwise direction, as in Fig. 2. This action wraps the fur round the silk and it should be repeated with additional fur until a sufficient length of the silk has been covered. Press the finger and thumb together firmly during the rolling, opening them at the end of each roll. I stress this point to make sure that you do not keep the finger and thumb together and just roll the fur backwards and forwards. It will be obvious that if rolling in one direction wraps the fur round the silk, rolling it back again will tend to unwrap it!

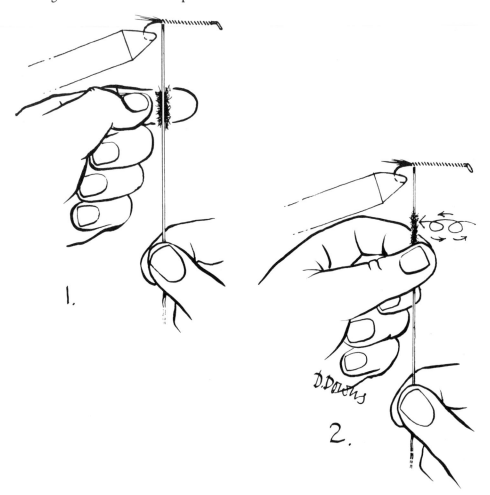

1.

2.

The dubbing should now look like that shown in Fig. 3, and is next wound towards the eye of the hook, not forgetting to leave enough space at the eye end for any wings and hackles that have to be tied on. The spacing of the winds of dubbing will regulate the thickness of the body, and it is usual to overlap them at the shoulders of the fly so that extra thickness is given at this point – see Fig. 4. It is customary to give a tinsel rib of some sort to a dubbing body, and this is, of course, tied in at the tail before starting on the dubbing. This adds to the durability of the body, and, by this method, it is possible to make bodies that are light and translucent, or thick and shaggy, which will put up with an almost unlimited amount of use. If a thick shaggy body is required, for a salmon fly for instance, it is still far better to apply only a little dubbing to the silk at a time, adding more bit by bit until a good thick 'barrel' is achieved. After this is wound round the hook shank, fibres can be pulled out from it with a dubbing needle to give the hackle effect which is often needed.

If one is using a fur which has to be cut from the skin before use, it should be cut so that the staple is as long as possible. If the fibres are cut off so that they are only about $\frac{1}{8}$ in. long, the difficulty of wrapping them round the silk is greatly increased.

It is also true that some furs are more easily applied than others – seal's fur, for instance, being more difficult than rabbit's or hare's. This is because the fibres of the seal's fur are stiffer and more springy than the others. The method to use is exactly the same for all furs, however, and it just means that the points I have emphasised should be followed more strictly when working with the difficult furs.

Among the many excellent suggestions given to me by Captain the Hon. R. Coke is his method of putting on dubbing bodies. This is particularly useful for those short-fibred dubbings which do not lend themselves easily to the spinning or rolling

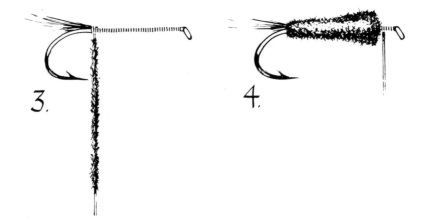

method described above. The procedure is as follows: the fly is formed to the point at which the dubbing is required, which would usually bring the tying silk to the tail. Another piece of well-waxed tying silk should now be tied in. Place a portion of the dubbing between the two silks, and then twist them together, embracing the dubbing. The silks and dubbing are then wound to form the body, care being taken to see that the silks stay twisted together. Finish off with the original tying silk and cut off the end of the subsidiary piece.

This brings me to a tip passed on to me by N. F. Bostock, an associate of the late G. E. M. Skues. Any material which has a twist given to it, as called for by this method, should be wound in the opposite direction to the twist. In other words, if the two silks are twisted together anti-clockwise to embrace the dubbing, they will not untwist when wound clockwise to form the body. This eliminates retwisting the silks while forming the body. It is also useful to remember this when making bodies of floss silk, which has a twist in it when taken from the reel. Winding it on in one direction will continue to twist the silk into a tight cord, whereas winding in the other will untwist it, so that a flat, well-shaped body is achieved. A small point, but a time saver.

List of feathers for trout flies

Bird	Feather	Use in fly tying
Bittern	Flank	Hackle of Matuka
Blackbird (cock)	Wing	Wings (Iron Blue Dun, etc.)
Blackbird (hen)	Wing	Wings (Greenwell)
Capercailzie	Wing	Wings (Alder)
Condor	Wing	Herls for bodies
Coot	Wing	Wings (Blue Wing Olive)
Crow	Wing	Wings (Butcher, etc.)
Corncrake (see Landrail)	Wing	Wings (Cinnamon Sedge, etc.)
	Breast	Hackles (Cowdung, etc.)
Duck, white	Wing	Wings (Coachman, etc.)
Egyptian goose	Breast	Wings and hackles of mayflies, etc.
French partridge (see Red leg)		
Golden pheasant	Crest (head)	Tails of lake- and sea-trout flies
	Tippet (neck)	Tails of lake- and sea-trout flies
Grouse	Neck	Hackles (Grouse Hackle, etc.)
	Tail	Wings (Grouse and Claret, etc.)
	Wing (covert)	Wings (Indian Yellow, etc.)
	Under-coverts	Hackles (Poult Bloa)
Guinea fowl	Neck (blue or white)	Hackles and whisks for nymphs
Heron	Breast (grey)	Herls for bodies
	Wing	Herls for bodies
Ibis	Breast	Tails of sea-trout and lake-trout flies
Jay	Lesser coverts (blue)	Throat hackles, etc.
Jungle cock	Neck	Sides and wings of sea-trout flies
Kingfisher	Back	Wings (Blue Kingfisher)
Landrail	Wing	Wings (Cinnamon Sedge, etc.)
Lapwing (substitute for Landrail)	Rump (brown)	Hackles (Cowdung, etc.)
Lapwing	Wing	Wings (Iron Blue Dun, etc.)
Magpie	Tail	Wing cases of beetles

Bird	Feather	Use in fly tying
Mallard duck (drake)	Grey breast and grey flank	Wings (Rube Wood, etc.) and wings and hackles of mayflies
	Wing quill (blue with white tip)	Wings (Butcher, Heckham, etc.)
	Wing quill (grey)	Wings (Wickham, etc.)
	Shoulder (brown)	Wings (Mallard and Claret, etc.)
	Underwing coverts (white)	Wings (Coachman)
Mandarin duck	Flank (brown)	Wings (Cahill, etc.)
	Breast (white)	Wings of fan-wing flies
Mavis thrush (substitute for Landrail)	Wing	Wings (Greenwell's Glory, etc.)
Moorhen (see Waterhen)		
Owl (brown)	Wing	Wings (Brown Owl, etc.)
Owl (light)	Wing	Wings (Owl, moths, etc.)
Ostrich	Wing and tail	Herls for bodies
Partridge	Back (brown)	Hackle (March Brown, etc.)
	Breast (grey)	Hackle (Hardies Favourite)
	Wing	Wings (Grannom, etc.)
	Tail (speckled and brown)	Wings (Cinnamon Sedge, etc.)
Peacock	Tail (eye)	Quill and herl bodies
	Quills (from eye tail)	Bodies (Blue Quill, etc.)
	Bronze herl (from stem of eye tail)	Bodies (Coch-y-Bonddu, etc.)
	Sword tail (green herl)	Wings of sea-trout flies (Alexandra, etc.)
Peewit (see Lapwing)		
Pheasant (cock)	Neck (red-brown)	Hackle (Bracken Clock)
	Wing	Wings (Nobbler, etc.)
	Tail	Tails of mayflies, etc., and herls (Pheasant Tail)
Pheasant (hen) (substitute for Bittern)	Flank	Hackle of Matuka
Pheasant (hen)	Wing	Wings (March Brown, etc.)
	Tail	Wings (Invicta, etc.)
Plover (see Lapwing)		
Poultry, chicken (cock)	Neck hackles	Hackles
	Saddle hackles	Wings of streamer flies, etc.
Poultry, chicken (hen)	Neck hackles	Hackles
	Lesser coverts	Wings (February Red, etc.)
	Wing quill (speckled)	Wings (Alder, etc.)
	Wing quill (plain)	Wings (sedges, etc.)

Bird	Feather	Use in fly tying
Red leg partridge (French partridge)	Breast	Hackle of mayflies
Rook	Wing	Wings (Butcher)
Rouen drake	Breast	For fan-wing mayflies
Snipe	Back	Hackles (Snipe and Purple)
	Wing	Wings (Blue Dun, etc.)
Starling	Breast and back	Hackles (Black Gnat, etc.)
	Wing	Wings (Olive Quill, etc.)
Swan	Shoulder	Herls for bodies
Summer duck	Flank (brown)	Wings (Cahill, etc.)
	Breast (white)	Wings of fan-wing flies
Teal duck	Breast	Fan-wing flies (Grizzly King, etc.)
	Breast and flank	Wings (Peter Ross, etc.)
	Wing quill (green)	Wings (Delius, etc.)
	Wing quill (grey)	Wings (Wickham, etc.)
Turkey	Tail (Cinnamon)	Herls for bodies
Turkey (dyed)	Tail	Herls for bodies
Waterhen	Wing	Wings and hackles (Waterhen Bloa, etc.)
Widgeon duck	Shoulder	Wings of sea-trout flies
Woodcock	Breast	Hackles (Woodcock and Claret, etc.)
	Wing	Wings (Woodcock and Green, etc.)
Wood duck (see Summer duck)		
Wild duck (see Mallard duck)		

List of feathers for salmon flies

Bird	Feather	Use in fly tying
Amherst pheasant	Tail	Wings
	Head (topping crest and tippet collar)	Tails and wings
Bustard florican	Wing	Wings
Bustard (speckled)	Wing	Wings
Bustard (white)	Shoulder	Wings
Chatterer (blue)	Breast or back	Sides and cheeks
Cock o' the rock	Breast	Sides, tails and veiling
Eagle	Leg	Hackles (Yellow Eagle, etc.)
Golden pheasant	Flank (red)	Hackles (Brown Fairy, etc.)
	Rump (yellow)	Hackles (Brown Fairy, etc.)
	Head (topping crest)	Tails and wings
	Neck (tippet collar)	Tails and wings
	Tail	Wings
Goose	Shoulder (soft)	Wings
Guinea fowl (gallena)	Breast and flank (spotted)	Throat hackles
	Wing	Wings
	Tail	Wings
Hen pheasant	Tail	Wings
Heron	Breast (grey)	Hackles (Grey Heron, etc.)
	Crest (black)	Hackles (Akroyd, etc.)
Ibis	Breast	Tails
Indian crow	Breast	Tails, cheeks and veiling
Jay	Lesser coverts (blue)	Throat hackles (Thunder and Lightning, etc.)
Jungle cock	Neck	Sides
Kingfisher (substitute for blue chatterer)	Back (blue)	Cheeks and sides
Macaw	Tail	Horns
Mallard duck (drake)	Grey flank (large)	Wings
	Brown shoulder	Wings

Bird	Feather	Use in fly tying
Mandarin duck	Flank (barred)	Wings and sides
	Wing (brown with white tip)	Wings (Akroyd, etc.)
Ostrich	Wing	Butts
Peacock	Sword tail	Wings
	Eye tail	Wings and bodies
	Wing	Wings
Partridge	Back (brown)	Hackle (March Brown)
Pintail duck	Flank	Wings
Poultry, chicken (cock)	Neck hackles	Hackles
Summer duck	Flank (barred)	Wings and sides
Swan	Shoulder (soft)	Wings
Teal duck	Flank	Wings and sides
Toucan	Breast	Sides, tails and veiling
Turkey	Quill (grey speckled)	Wings
Turkey (substitute for speckled bustard)	Quill (oak brown)	Wings
Turkey	Rumps (white tip)	Wings
	Rumps (cinnamon)	Wings
Turkey (substitute for peacock wing)	Tail (buff mottled)	Wings
Turkey	Tail (white tip)	Wings
	Tail (cinnamon)	Wings
	Tail (brown mottled)	Wings
Vulturine gallena	Breast (striped)	Wings (Elver Fly)
	Back (blue)	Hackle (Elver Fly)
Widgeon duck	Shoulder	Wings, sides and hackles
	Neck	Hackles
Wood duck (see Summer duck)		

Fly-tying terminology

Bi-visible flies These are designed to improve the visibility of flies to both angler and fish, particularly when using dark flies in poor light. It merely entails adding a white or light-coloured hackle to the front of the hackle called for in the dressing. In other words, if a white hackle is wound in front of the hackle used on the Red Palmer, the fly would then be called a Red Palmer Bi-visible.

Bobbin holder A tool for holding a whole reel of silk during tying, which dispenses the silk as required.

Detached body The body of an artificial fly, complete in itself, tied onto the hook shank, but separate from it.

Dry fly A fly so dressed that it will remain afloat when in contact with the water.

Dubbing See Fur bodies.

Dubbing needle Used to pick out fur fibres on a 'dubbed' body, to simulate legs, feelers, etc.

Fluorescence Some fly-tying materials are treated to have this property – the ability to reflect light rays during the hours of daylight – and are useful during dull days and heavy water conditions. It is not possible to get dark shades, such as black, and only pastel shades of the primary colours, or variations of them, can be achieved. Manufactured fibres such as nylon react very well to this treatment, but natural materials such as hackles can be quite effective also.

Fur bodies These are formed by twisting or 'dubbing' furs onto the tying silk, and then winding them round the hook shank to form the body of the fly.

Hackle Feather wound round the hook shank to represent the legs or wings of a fly.

Hackle pliers Used to grip the tip of the hackle when winding it.

Hair bodies These are formed by using the stiffish body hairs of the common deer. They are spun on to form a 'hackle' which is then cut to any desired body shape. This method is used not only because bulky bodies can be made up, but also because of the extremely good floatability of this type of body.

Herls Short fibres or 'flue' which stand out from individual feather fibres or quills. When these fibres or quills are wound round the hook shank, the flue stands out at right-angles, giving a certain amount of translucence to the solid body. Peacock and ostrich tail feather fibres are the two best examples of herls, but fibres from wing quills and tail feathers of many other birds are also used – heron, condor, goose and swan being very popular.

Irons This is the old Scottish name for salmon-fly hooks and is now in general use to describe any type of hook.

Low-water flies Very lightly dressed salmon flies, the wing-tips of which are dressed well forward of the bend of the hook. They are used in summer or low-water conditions with the 'greased line' method, so called because the whole of the line and the leader – to within 18 in. of the fly – is greased, to ensure that the fly does not sink very far below the surface.

Mallard feathers for wings One often comes across this term in the dressing of a fly, but as the mallard supplies so many feathers for wings, some difficulty may be experienced in deciding which one to choose. The best thing I can do here is give the names of the best-known flies which use different types of mallard feathers.

Bronze mallard shoulder feathers Mallard and Claret and all the other Mallard series of flies. Connemara Black, Golden Olive, Fiery Brown, Thunder and Lightning, Blue Charm, and nearly all other salmon flies which have mixed wings.

Grey mallard flank feathers This is a grey speckled feather similar to teal flank, but with much lighter markings. It is used for John Spencer, Queen of Waters, Grizzly King, Professor, and as a substitute for teal and pintail feathers in many salmon flies.

Grey mallard quill feathers These are the wing primary feathers, and can be used for nearly any fly which calls for a grey wing, particularly in the larger sizes, i.e. Silver Saltoun, Wickham's Fancy, Blae and Black, etc.

Blue/white tipped mallard quill feathers These also come from the wing, the blue part of the quill being used for one of the best known of all flies – the Butcher. Strips taken from the white tip of the feather are used for Heckham and Red (and all the others of the Heckham series) McGinty, Jock, and, in fact, any fly which has a wing with a white tip. This includes small and low-water salmon flies where a white-tipped turkey tail feather would be too large.

Married fibres Fibres taken from different feathers and then joined together to form one whole wing section. Used mainly for mixed- and built-wing salmon flies.

Palmer fly Any fly which has the hackle wound from shoulder to tail. A fly so dressed is usually referred to as 'tied Palmer'.

Parachute fly This term is used for flies with the hackle wound in a horizontal plane instead of round the hook shank.

Quill *Body:* usually formed by one of the fibres from a peacock's tail, after the flue has been stripped from it. Strips cut from the centre quill of tail or wing quill feathers with a knife can also be used. *Wings:* when a dressing calls for a wing from a 'quill', this means that the feather fibres from the quill are used for the wing.

Ribs These can be formed of silk, herls or tinsels. On trout flies they are usually meant to simulate the segmentations of insect bodies, whereas on salmon flies their function is to strengthen the body material and protect any body hackle which is used.

Silk bodies Strands of silk, usually floss, wound directly onto the hook shank to form the body.

Tail See Whisks.

Tail feather When a dressing calls for a wing or part of a wing from a tail feather, this means that the feather fibres from the tail are used. The Grouse and Green uses feather fibres from the grouse tail.

Tandem hooks Two or more hooks whipped to gut, nylon monofilament, or wire, in line with each other. Used mostly for sea- and lake-trout lures, sometimes referred to as Demons and Terrors. The popular Worm Fly is usually tied on a two-hook tandem.

Teal feathers for wings As with the mallard, the teal supplies several feathers for wings. When a fly has a black-and-white barred feather for the wings, it is the breast or flank feather of the teal which is used. Such flies are Peter Ross, Teal and Green, Teal and Blue, and all the others of the Teal series. The grey feathers of the wing can be used for such patterns as Wickham's Fancy or any other largish pattern requiring a grey wing.

Tinsel Strips of flat metal and strands of silk covered with metal. Used for whole bodies or just for ribbing. When in doubt, use a flat tinsel for a whole body, and the covered silk tinsel for ribbing.

Tinsel bodies Bodies made of metal strip wound the length of the hook shank, used to impart 'flash' to a fly, particularly those flies which are supposed to resemble a small fish.

Tube flies Flies which have the body hackle and wings (if any) tied on to a length of plastic or metal tubing. The hook is supplied by tying a double or treble hook to a length of gut, and passing it through the tube.

Tying silk Fine natural silk, by which all materials are tied to the hook.

Wax This enables the tying silk to grip the materials firmly while the fly is being tied. Solid or liquid types can be used.

Wet fly A fly so dressed that it will sink when cast.

Whip finish The best method of finishing off a fly. It consists of two or three turns of the tying silk laid over the end of the silk before it is pulled tight.

Whip finisher A tool designed to simplify the application of the whip finish to the fly. It is only suitable for this purpose and cannot apply whip finishes to rods, hooks to gut, or any other article which has a projection beyond the actual whip finish.

Whisks Fibres of feathers used to form the tail. If material such as wool or silk is used, it is more often referred to as a 'tag' instead of a tail.

Wings The following is a list of the various types of wings used on trout and salmon flies.

Wet fly A flat wing sloping back over the body of the fly.

Double split-wing dry fly Formed of two sections each, taken from a pair of matched wing quills and tied in so that the tips point outwards.

Fan wings Formed of two small breast feathers, usually from the mallard drake, tied in to curve outwards.

Advanced wing Term used when the wings slopes over the eye of the fly instead of the body. Can be a flat wing or a double split wing.

Down wing Used for dry flies which simulate the sedge group, stone flies and alder flies.

Rolled wings These consist of a roll of feather fibres taken from a wing quill or tail. They are used for the down-wing types mentioned above, and for some well-known types of North Country upright-winged dry flies.

Upright wing Any wing that stands upright from the body of the fly. They can be double, split wings, fan wings, rolled wings, hackle-point wings, etc.

Bunch wings Wings formed by a bunch of fibres cut from any feather. They can be tied upright, low over the body, advanced or split.

Split wings Any wings that have their points separated.

Hackle-point wings Almost self-explanatory. The tips of hackles are used to form the wings, two for most patterns, four for mayflies.

Spent wings Wings tied so that they lie flat on the water when the fly is cast – imitating the spent fly. Hackle points or hackle fibres are the most popular of this type.

Hackle-fibre wings Similar to 'bunch wings' in so far as a bunch of hackle fibres is used for the wings.

Shaving-brush wings Hair or feather fibres tied in so that they point forward over the eye of the hook in line with the shank. Down-eyed hooks should be used to facilitate the tying on of the leader, or the tying silk should be wound so as to form a slight split down the centre of the wing.

Hair wings Wings formed of animal fur fibres. Invariably down wings or wings of the shaving-brush type.

Streamer wings Wings formed of whole hackles or long strips of other feathers, the tips of which project well beyond the bend of the hook.

Strip wings A term used for salmon-fly wings which are made of strips taken from one type of feather only.

Whole-feather wings Term used when a whole feather, or two whole feathers back to back, form the wing of the fly.

Mixed wings Wings that are formed from the fibres of several different feathers, 'married' together to form single whole sections.

Herl wings Wings that are formed with the feathers normally used for herl bodies. The Alexandra is the best-known example.

Wing cases The 'hump' incorporated in the dressings of nymphs and beetle imitations to simulate the wing housing. Wing cases are usually formed of feather fibres tied in at one point, folded down onto the body and then tied in at another point. If fur or silk is used for the body, this should be thickened between these two points to accentuate the hump.

Varnish This is applied to the final turns or whip finish of the fly, to prevent the silk unravelling during use. Clear varnish is usually used for dry flies, while spirit and coloured varnishes are used for wet flies and salmon flies.

It is as well to have a way of ensuring that bottles of varnish are not knocked over whilst actually tying. An accident of this nature could ruin many hours of work, or make valuable items of material unusable. A simple stand capable of taking a selection of varnishes and thinners was designed by Peter Deane and is illustrated on page 109.

Index

Note: Numbers in italics refer to Colour Plates.

143